THE **AMAZING** BOOK OF **MAZES**

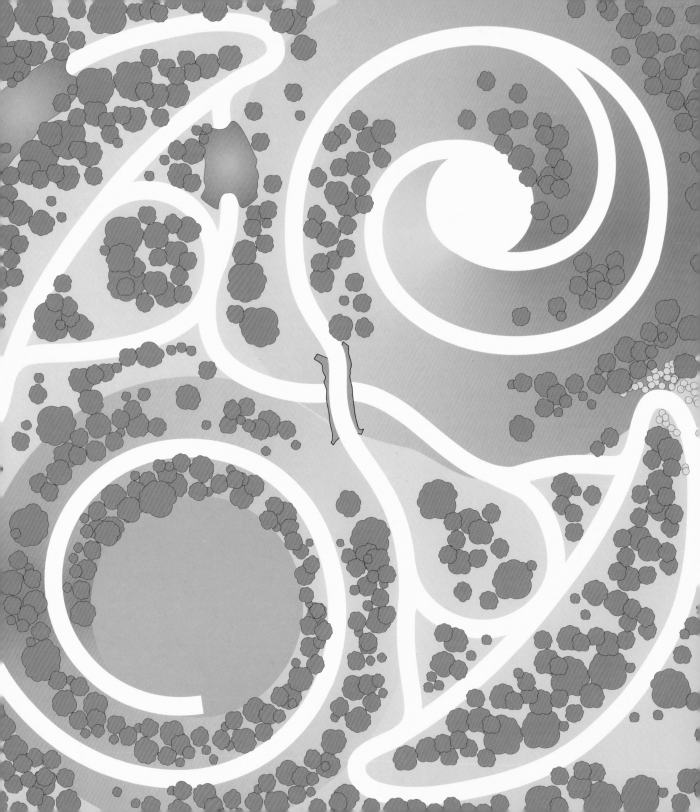

ADRIAN FISHER

THE **AMAZING** BOOK OF **MAZES**

ABRAMS, NEW YORK

To my wife Marie

who shares our joyful livelihood

this book is most affectionately dedicated

Abrams jacket design: E.Y. Lee

Library of Congress Cataloging-in-Publication Data

Fisher, Adrian.
 The amazing book of mazes / by Adrian Fisher.
  p. cm.
 Includes bibliographical references and index.
 ISBN-13: 978-0-8109-4311-7 (hardcover)
 ISBN-10: 0-8109-4311-5 (hardcover)
 1. Maze puzzles. I. Title.
 GV1507.M3F57 2006
 793.73'8—dc22
                2006015743

Printed and bound in China
10 9 8 7 6 5 4 3 2 1

HNA
harry n. abrams, inc.
a subsidiary of La Martinière Groupe
115 West 18th Street
New York, NY 10011
www.hnabooks.com

CONTENTS

INTRODUCTION

The archetype of a maze is universally familiar, lost in the mists of everyone's childhood memories. Often this may be no more than the idea of a confusing network of pathways. Different countries and cultures have different concepts of a maze. In Britain, the classic form is a hedge maze, 'like the one at Hampton Court'. In Japan people think of wooden panel mazes, following the great Japanese maze craze of the 1980s. In the United States, cornfield maize mazes are currently the most familiar form.

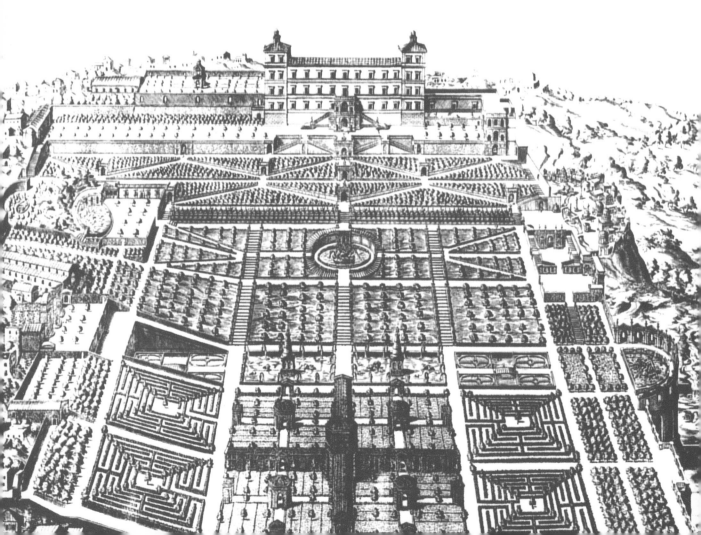

Underlying these differing forms, the same
puzzle maze elements are present: a defined start;
a complex network of paths, with junctions, choices
and dead ends; twisting and deceptive alleys weaving
between tall barriers; and finally an elusive goal
to be reached. Yet in our own generation, the
puzzle maze is going through such a renaissance
of innovation and explosive growth around the
world that it is no overstatement to say that we are
living through the greatest 'Golden Age' of mazes.

The words 'maze' and 'labyrinth' have distinctly
different meanings, though confusingly they are
often used interchangeably. Puzzle mazes have
existed for only about 500 years, whereas
labyrinths, from which they are descended,
go back at least 4,000 years. A labyrinth implies
a single path and aspects of ritual, while a maze
is a puzzle, with junctions and choices.

Labyrinths throughout history have been rich
in content and symbolism, and over the millennia,
in different cultures and civilizations, they have
represented journeys of conquest, sieges of cities,

Labyrinths, such as the medieval Christian example shown
right at Saint-Quentin parish church in France, often have a
spiritual underpinning, whereas hedge mazes – for example,
left, at the Villa d'Este in Italy – began within princely and
ducal gardens as part of their display of wealth and power.

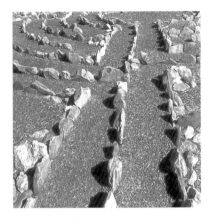  

pilgrimages, the rites of passage into adulthood, death and rebirth, and that linear thread of time, the 'Path of Life'. Religious and communal processions have trod their pathways. Their coils have offered protection against evil spirits (which apparently cannot easily go round corners), and have symbolized the female womb, with the journey of the male seed penetrating and fertilizing the egg, and then emerging again, newborn.

The earliest labyrinth design was the 'Classical Labyrinth'; it is usually circular, and has seven rings of paths traced between eight rings of barriers. Such patterns were laid out with rings of stone or cut in turf, carved on wooden door lintels, and appeared across many civilizations and throughout many centuries. The Classical Labyrinth design even appeared on the coins of Knossos on the island of Crete, dating to the third to first centuries BC.

The Romans introduced a second distinctive labyrinth design with four-fold symmetry, which was laid indoors as mosaic flooring. Over sixty examples, some highly impressive, have been found all across the Roman Empire, from Cyprus in the east to Portugal in the west, and from Yorkshire,

England, in the north to Libya in the south. Most were square and portrayed walled cities, and at their centres often depicted the scene of Theseus slaying the Minotaur.

The Classical design continued to be ideal for outdoor use, made with rings of stones and boulders, or cut into turf; this design spread across Northern Europe from Roman times onwards. The labyrinths often bore the names of famous ancient cities, most often Troy (and variations such as Trojaburg and Troy Town) but also such names as Babylon, Nineveh, Jericho, Jerusalem and Constantinople. The cities of Troy and Jericho suffered two of the great sieges of ancient times. They both had seemingly impregnable walls, which only yielded to deception or supernatural power.

The overcoming of the walls of Troy involved their partial destruction, brought about by the greed of the Trojans and their eagerness to bring the wooden horse into the city. The walls of Jericho 'yielded' after a ritual procession involving seven circuits, which precipitated an earthquake. From their earliest days, labyrinths were associated with the spiritual forces of good and evil.

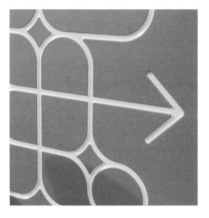  

In India, 'Classical' labyrinth designs are often called *Kote*, meaning 'fort'. In a manuscript of the Indian epic *Ramayana*, dated to about AD 1045, a labyrinth illustrates the castle of the demon Ravana. The story tells how Ravana abducts Sita, the wife of Rama, and takes her to Lanka. Rama, with an army of apes, attacks the labyrinth-castle of Lanka, kills Ravana and frees his wife. After the victory, Rama and Sita leave Lanka in Ravana's chariot, significantly making seven circuits around the fortress. Further east in Sumatra, labyrinths are carved in the wooden lintels above doorways, to keep out evil spirits.

Another great labyrinth style is the 'Medieval Christian' labyrinth with eleven rings of paths, which double back on each of the four axes to portray a distinctive Christian cross. These first appeared in manuscripts, followed by a number of examples in the indoor stone pavements of the great medieval abbeys and cathedrals of the twelfth to sixteenth centuries. The oldest surviving and most famous pavement labyrinth, built in the early 1200s, can be found at Chartres Cathedral in France. Those at Amiens Cathedral, Bayeux Cathedral, Saint-Quentin parish church and the church of San Vitale in Ravenna still survive; others in the French cathedrals of Arras, Chambéry, Poitiers, Rheims and Sens no longer exist.

Puzzle mazes have a different pedigree, originating as part of the formal and ornamental patterns of gardens surrounding great European houses, villas, palaces, castles and châteaux. Regular patterns, order and symmetry provided the structure for these extensive gardens. Mazes with barriers of tall hedges began to appear towards the end of the sixteenth century. In 1599 the maze at Nonsuch Palace, Surrey, England, was described as 'being set round with high plants so that one could neither go over nor through them'. Perhaps the most famous puzzle maze in the world was created at Hampton Court Palace in 1690. In France, garden labyrinths at Chantilly, Choisy-le-Roi and the Palace of Versailles had confusing patterns and spirals, rather than the tight designs that we would recognize as modern puzzle mazes. The Versailles example

contained a series of allegorical fountains based on Aesop's *Fables*; but while this provided a themed storyline, there was nothing symbolic about the design. At this stage, the topic was being driven by horticulturalists rather than by artistic designers.

The idea of using a maze to portray an image was first suggested in the sixteenth century by the Paduan architect Francesco Segala, who created woodcut images in maze form in his book *Libro de laberinti de Franc. Segalla Padoano Scultore et Architettore*, a copy of which can be found in the Vatican Library. His maze images included a man, horseman, jester, dog, dolphin, snail, crab and sailing ship; implied by its title, the book probably contains many more similar images. He used the internal lines of each maze to reinforce its image in an illustrative way. There is no record of any of these ever being created in the landscape; their intricate designs would have involved path lengths of over a mile, too large for formal gardens.

Gradually the mathematical possibilities of mazes began to be explored. Earl Stanhope's maze at

Chevening House in England in the 1820s was the first to use 'islands' to detach the goal from the perimeter hedge, and thus defeat the hand-on-wall method of solving puzzle mazes. In the mid-nineteenth century, tastes in private gardens were tending back towards formality, and hedges, topiary and puzzle hedge mazes once more came into vogue. The 'Italianate' style of gardening became popular in England during the 1830s and 1840s. Hedge mazes in this style were created at Shrublands Hall and Somerleyton Hall, both in Suffolk, as well as at Bridge End Gardens in

Saffron Walden, while the most notable of all was commissioned by Prince Albert for London's Great Exhibition of 1851: an Italianate hedge maze created by William Nesfield within the Royal Horticultural Society's display garden, on a site now occupied by the South Kensington museums. Mazes increased in popularity across London at places of public entertainment, such as the Ranelagh Gardens, Vauxhall Gardens, and Beulah Spa.

Meanwhile, the maze idea also began to appear indoors and on a smaller scale. Mirror mazes first appeared towards the end of the nineteenth century,

and several appeared within a few years of each other on both sides of the Atlantic. The earliest evidence of a mirror maze is a photograph on a stereo viewer card, captioned as 'Labyrinth of Pillars, Palace of the Sultan, Constantinople'; the card is dated 1889. This may have been a temporary exhibit since nothing else is known about it. The world's oldest surviving mirror maze is situated on Petrin Hill, Prague, in the Czech Republic, and was originally set up for the Jubilee Exhibition of 1891. Five years later, an impressive mirror maze was created for the Swiss national exhibition in Geneva;

it was a glorious recreation of the Alhambra Palace in Spain, with decorated arches, a cloistered courtyard, and the illusion of an orchard; in 1899, it was transported and re-opened at the Glacier Gardens, Lucerne, Switzerland, where it remains open to this day. Gustav Castan of Berlin, Germany, filed a patent for a mirror maze in 1895, and created a mirror maze and house of horror in the same year at Fort Edmonton Park in Alberta, Canada. Mirror mazes featured in several world fairs and expositions in North America: the first was in 1901, at the World Fair at Buffalo, New York State; this was followed at the St Louis World Fair in 1904 by a Crystal Maze featuring a crystal mirror or glass labyrinth with over 150 French plate curved mirrors which gave absurd, grotesque reflections; there was also a mirror maze at the 1939 New York World Fair in Corona Park, Long Island.

However, the social and economic upheaval of two world wars depressed the scope for mazes, and led to neglect of existing gardens. For half a century it was difficult to maintain gardens, let alone develop them, and many existing hedge mazes were abandoned while few new ones were created. Thus when the subject began to be revisited from the 1970s onwards, a new generation of designers approached mazes with fresh and innovative ideas, and the past thirty to forty years have seen some of the greatest changes in the history of maze design. Until the late twentieth century, puzzle maze designs had been geometric and abstract; then, in 1975, Randoll Coate created the world's first symbolic maze, in the shape of a giant footprint in a private garden in Gloucestershire. As well as its distinctive

outline shape, he worked images and symbols into the pattern of the internal hedges; and he also made it work as a challenging puzzle maze. He created further symbolic mazes at the Château de Beloeil in Belgium (1977) and Varmlands Saby in Sweden (1979). The Varmlands Maze contains two layers of superimposed imagery (one of the Garden of Eden, the other of the Minotaur) both using the same rows of hedges, and is one of his most remarkable achievements. Independently, in 1978, Greg Bright created a highly influential hedge maze at Longleat House. With its sinuous paths, gigantic spirals and numerous bridges, it broke away from the predictable geometry and symmetry of conventional hedge mazes, and its size also set a new world record for the path length of hedge mazes.

My own career as a maze-maker began as a boy designing puzzles, and then later on creating a full-size hedge maze in my parents' garden in Bournemouth. In 1979 Randoll Coate and I founded Minotaur Designs, and together until 1986 we created fifteen symbolic mazes, several times in

association with Graham Burgess, including the Beatles Maze (see p. 216) and the Leeds Castle hedge maze (p. 49–51). I then founded Adrian Fisher Mazes Ltd, and by 2005 the company had created over 500 mazes, and was designing at a rate of 90 mazes a year.

Several new forms of maze construction have appeared over the past twenty to thirty years. Between 1984 and 1988, Stuart Landsborough from New Zealand pioneered a craze across Japan for wooden fence mazes of astonishing complexity and scale; his 22 mazes were among the most

ambitious, and within four years a total of 220 were built, though most no longer exist. His own fence maze at Wanaka, South Island, has been continuously open to the public since 1973.

A few years later in America, Jean Houston conducted a labyrinth workshop which was attended by the Reverend Dr Lauren Artress from Grace Cathedral, San Francisco. Lauren was so inspired that she travelled to France, visited Chartres Cathedral and experienced its famous pavement labyrinth. She returned to Grace Cathedral and in December 1991 used a canvas labyrinth painted to the Chartres design for their New Year's Eve service. She founded Veriditas as a Christian charity dedicated to using labyrinths for spiritual purposes, and travelled widely around America, even taking her portable labyrinth into jails to reach convicts. In 1995, a permanent pavement labyrinth was laid outside Grace Cathedral, and now across America over 400 church labyrinths have been created both outdoors and indoors, further encouraged by the formation of the Labyrinth Society.

In the popular imagination, the larger the maze is, the more complex it must be. While this is not always true, there is something rather exciting about truly giant mazes. In 1993, Don Frantz and I created the world's first cornfield Maize Maze in Pennsylvania, and established the potential for gigantic puzzle mazes with several miles of paths. Adrian Fisher Mazes pioneered the genre including designing all the plans, and by 2004 were creating over 50 maize mazes a year across Europe and North America. We set six Guinness World Records for ever larger corn mazes, three times in America and three times in Britain. Other corn maze design companies started up in America, creating further mazes each year; the combined effect was that some three million visitors explored about four hundred cornfield mazes across America in 2005.

While, as we saw earlier, the mirror maze had enjoyed great popularity as an exposition feature and fairground attraction in the late nineteenth century, in 1991 the format was revived when we created the Magical Mirror Maze at Wookey Hole Caves. This mirror maze was on a scale never previously attempted, and immensely disorientating since the mirrors are so far apart that that visitors cannot touch both sides at once. This proved to be the first of a new generation of mirror mazes. We pioneered the use of multiple 'episodes' to convey a storyline, seemingly random mirror layouts to create non-architectural effects, sensational gags and special effects, and developed modular forms of construction for rapid installation even in awkwardly shaped buildings. Today, we have installed mirror mazes across Britain, France,

Germany, the Netherlands, the United States, the Middle East, India and Japan.

Mazes pervade our modern culture far beyond indoor or landscape attractions. Mazes have featured in movies including *The Lady from Shanghai*, *The Shining*, *The Man with the Golden Gun*, and *Harry Potter and the Goblet of Fire*. Many computer games have maze-like characteristics, from the enigmatic 'Myst', to PacMan, and Lara Croft and the Temple of Doom. Websites such as Andrea Gilbert's www.clickmazes.com provide interactive online mazes on the internet. Many of the most impressive puzzles created by Bill Ritchie's company ThinkFun have strong maze influences, including Rush Hour, Lunar Lockout, Tipover and River Crossing. Maze puzzles such as Navigati are joining crosswords and Su Doku within the puzzle pages of newspapers and magazines. Even now, more ambitious physical mazes are being planned, including mirror mazes as complete walk-through themed environments, and hedge mazes such as that in the Sigurta Gardens in Italy with its collection of fine antique stone carvings within its exit tunnel.

Future trends are always difficult to predict, but considering the current interest in mazes it is exciting to consider what might happen next. One recent trend has been the emergence of hybrid activities that used to be kept separate, so that education and entertainment are found together, as are entertainment and shopping, entertainment and eating, and religion and entertainment. Museums and galleries of all kinds are redefining themselves as places to have experiences, events, parties and social occasions, just as much as a place to view collections. Thus mazes and labyrinths are now appearing in shopping malls, city centres, waterfronts, museums, safari parks, zoos and aquariums, churches and schools. Location-based destinations will increasingly provide real and actual experiences, rather than screen-based simulations which can be installed in every home. Full-size mazes are ideal for 'Actual Reality' instead of Virtual Reality. Yet we can still expect some of the most fantastical mazes and multiple-outcome maze adventures on screen, whether the smaller screens of computers and home televisions, or wide screens at the movies,

as computer simulation software becomes ever
more sophisticated.

No doubt new, ever larger, mazes will continue to
be reported in the Guinness Book of World Records;
but beyond a certain size what matters with mazes is
the quality of the experience, the storyline adventure,
and entering into the spirit of a themed or quest or
journey. Thus the state-of-the-art of modern maze
design comes full circle to the earliest role of ancient
labyrinths, as a highly relevant social experience –
though nowadays more for a family or group of
friends than a village community.

VERTICAL MAZES

Ask most people what a puzzle maze looks like and they will describe one with a complicated network of vertical barriers. While, as this book shows, mazes can be constructed in many different ways, the vertical maze is the most common form, whether built from hedges, stone, brick, fencing, panels, grasses or maize cornstalks. Apart from blocking our path, the barriers in vertical mazes also block the view, thus building up the desire to discover what is forbidden and out of sight...

HEDGE MAZES

Hedge mazes are the garden form of the art, with the sheer simplicity of vertical planted barriers with level paths between. Yet they display such a diversity of location, scale and material, that almost every example is unique.

Hedge mazes are not only among the largest garden features, but they are also the least practical or 'productive'. They are explicitly for fun and pleasure, for social entertaining, as places for flirting and courtship, and as an expression of wealth and political power.

Formal gardens have been created by many civilizations over thousands of years, enclosed for protection against foraging by wild animals, and to provide shelter for better cultivation. Yet the idea of creating a puzzle maze with tall hedges did not occur until recent European garden history. The earliest evidence of a maze using shrubs is ironically the record of the destruction of one in Paris in 1431. Made often from clipped yew, box or privet (but early on also from plants such as hyssop, thyme and lavender), these early mazes were only knee-high. By 1494 'a knot in a garden, called a

above Plan of the Dream of Poliphilo maze at the Château de Thoiry, France
opposite The maze at Chatsworth House, England

mase' had become a common phrase in England. Early garden mazes had low plant-filled barriers, and were decorative rather than puzzles. Like knot gardens, they formed attractive patterns that could be appreciated close up, or from a raised surrounding walk or window.

Hedge mazes began to proliferate during the late Renaissance, especially in Italy, since they could be seen as intellectual as well as beautiful. Scholars noted the Roman enthusiasm for labyrinths in mosaic, and linked these designs with descriptions of gardens using low box plants by Pliny and other Roman writers. Four low shrub mazes were planted in the 1560s at the gardens of Villa d'Este, in Tivoli, Italy.

Mazes with barriers of tall hedges began to appear in England in the sixteenth century. At Theobalds in Hertfordshire, Lord Burghley had a garden hedge maze constructed about 1560, but it was 'demolish'd by the rebels' during the English Civil War, according to John Evelyn in his *Memoirs*. In 1599 the maze at Nonsuch Palace, Surrey, was described as being 'set round with high plants so that one could neither go over nor through them'. Despite having tall hedges that concealed the design, there is no evidence that either of these mazes contained junctions or choices, and Theobolds was certainly 'unicursal': no one had yet seized on the idea of using the tall hedges to conceal a puzzle.

The seventeenth century was something of a golden age for formally planned gardens, and this was reflected in a profusion of mazes. However, the late seventeenth century saw the rise of the 'block'-type maze, especially in the Netherlands, France and England. In these the hedges were no longer of uniform thickness, but instead had winding paths penetrating large blocks of shrubs and offered a

diverting walk from one hidden feature to another. The Labyrinth of Versailles, constructed by J. Hardouin-Mansart for Louis XIV, was the most notable example. The oldest surviving maze in Germany is at Altjessnitz, in Sachsen-Anhalt, originally planted in hornbeam in 1750. The earliest surviving hedge maze in Italy was planted in *c.* 1688 at the Villa Barbarigo, Val Sanzibio. In 1691, two hedge mazes were created at Kromeriz in the Czech Republic. At about the same time William III of England built the famous hedge maze at Hampton

above This early parterre in Chudleigh, Devon, England, is typical of the simple geometric patterns that preceded low shrub mazes, which in time became full-height hedge mazes. *opposite* A speculative design for a maze by Flemish artist Jan Vredeman De Vries , from *Hortum Viridariorumque Elegantes et Mumultiplicis Formae*, 1583

Court Palace, with junctions, choices, dead ends, islands of hedges and a central goal. William had previously created a hedge maze in 1682 at Het Loo Palace in Holland. The Hampton Court maze has inspired hedge mazes throughout the world,

below The hedge maze at Sorgvliet Castle in the Netherlands in the 1690s was evidently a remarkable spectacle, and even allowing for graphic exaggeration, the central mound is massive, surrounded by five concentric circular rings of paths.

opposite This hedge maze with elaborate gates and central pavilion was created by Jesuit missionaries in Beijing in the late seventeenth century. Why they did this is unclear: perhaps to recreate a familiar garden environment so far from Europe, or perhaps the allegory of The Path of Life was in their minds (although at that time puzzle mazes with junctions and decisions were not used to explore spiritual ideas such as Choice and Free Will). There is no evidence that it was used as a direct part of their missionary work.

including many copies of its distinctive trapezoid design, with varying degrees of faithfulness.

By the eighteenth century, hedge mazes were being created across Europe. In 1720 at Villa Pisani, the famous hedge maze with its distinctive central tower and twin external spiral staircases, was planted near Stra in northern Italy. In Denmark in the 1730s, a rectangular version of the Hampton Court design was laid out at Egeskov Castle. In France, a hedge maze was created in the Jardin des Plantes in Paris around 1734. In Austria, a geometric hedge maze was planted in the 1750s within the formal gardens of the Schönbrunn Palace in Vienna. In 1791, the Laberint d'Horta was created in

Barcelona, and remains Spain's most distinguished hedge maze, with its distinctive circle of eight tall arches of clipped cypress.

America's first hedge maze was created in *c.* 1805, as a living vine maze at Harmony, Pennsylvania; it was planted by the Harmonists, a dissident religious group from Germany, to reflect their spiritual beliefs. Back in England, in the 1820s the 4th Lord Stanhope planted a maze at Chevening, to a design by the 2nd Earl who was an eminent mathematician. This was the first maze that detached the perimeter hedge from the goal, thus defeating the 'hand-on-wall' method of solving mazes. In the 1840s, the 'Italianate' style of gardening became popular in England, influencing

hedge mazes at Shrublands Hall and Bridge End Gardens in Saffron Walden (1839). Somerleyton Hall (1846) has a central oriental pavilion within its maze, and a replica was planted at Worden Park, Lancashire (1886). A Chinese influence prevailed at Woburn Abbey, whose maze with its painted pavilion is in the private gardens.

Victorian hedge mazes were built in many English public parks. This enthusiasm spread across the English-speaking world, with Australia's earliest hedge maze in the Ballarat Botanic Gardens in 1862, followed by Belair Park, Adelaide, in 1886, and Geelong 1896. In India, a hedge maze was created in the 1880s in the gardens of the Governor's Palace near Calcutta. In Belgium, a hedge maze appeared at

above, left and right A view and plan of the maze at Egeskov Castle, Denmark, planted in *c.* 1730, and based on the design of the maze at Hampton Court (though rectangularized).

opposite Vizcaya Gardens Maze, Miami, Florida, 1916, the oldest surviving hedge maze in the United States.

the Château de Loppem in 1873. In America, there were hedge mazes at the Hotel del Monte in Monterey (*c.* 1880), and the Rafael Hotel in San Rafael (*c.* 1887), both in California. Also in California, a circular hedge maze complete with central pagoda was created in Piedmont Park,

Oakland, around 1900; another circular maze was planted in 1902 in Centennial Park, Nashville, Tennessee. The oldest surviving hedge maze in America is at the Vizcaya Gardens near Miami, Florida, which was planted in 1916.

From 1914, the social and economic upheaval of two world wars resulted in the neglect of existing gardens, and for half a century it was difficult to maintain gardens let alone develop them. Many

below The public maze next to the 'Parthenon', Centennial Park, Nashville, Tennessee, planted *c.* 1902, destroyed 1930.

existing mazes became overgrown and forgotten. Occasionally hedge mazes were established or restored between the wars, such as at Colonial Williamsburg, Virginia, in 1935, but these were very much the exception.

The modern renaissance in hedge mazes began in 1978 at Longleat House, when Greg Bright designed the world's largest permanent hedge maze (as measured by path length), using six bridges

above The maze at Piedmont Park, Oakland, California, from around 1900, had a distinctive three-level pagoda at the centre.

and curving paths to create some two miles of unprecedented puzzlement. Around the same time, the late Randoll Coate had begun designing symbolic hedge mazes, starting in 1975 with 'Imprint' in Oxfordshire, followed by 'Pyramid' at the Château de Beloeil in Belgium in 1977, and 'Creation' at

opposite Jubilee Maze, Symonds Yat, Herefordshire, England

Varmlands Saby in Sweden in 1979. Between 1979 and 1986 I worked with him on fifteen mazes, including several of the hedge mazes illustrated here – Leeds Castle, the Marlborough Maze at Blenheim Palace, and the Alice-in-Wonderland Maze, among others. The outline shapes of symbolic mazes are powerful and compelling, especially when portraying a spectacular image – such as that of a dragon, tortoise, or giant footprint. The lines of hedges within the maze can also convey hidden messages on a huge scale, perhaps best viewed from the air.

Since then I have worked on another thirty public hedge mazes around the world including those at Legoland, Scone Palace, Edinburgh Zoo, the Château de Thoiry and Three Lands Point. Along the way I have been able to introduce innovations such as wrought iron maze gates, central towers, and multiple bridges to give the maze three dimensions. Water features in mazes have proved particularly popular, especially 'Walk-Through Parting Waterfalls' and 'Foaming Fountain Gates'. Microelectronics can be used to create interactive encounters, such as within the hedge maze at the Château de Thoiry. In America, modern hedge mazes have been created at many different places; perhaps the most interesting is the one at the new Getty Museum, Los Angeles, which has paths of water, and is intended to be viewed from above.

Hedge mazes are appearing in an increasingly wide range of visitor destinations, from theme parks such as Disneyland Paris to zoos, botanical gardens, historic houses and gardens. However, with thoughts turning to gardening in longer and increasingly active lives, another modern trend is for hedge mazes in extensive private gardens, where the latest maintenance techniques, lighting and electronic wizardry are transforming this most traditional of forms of the maze-maker's art.

HATFIELD HOUSE MAZE
HERTFORDSHIRE, ENGLAND

This delightful maze has been designed to be seen rather than walked in; indeed, the hedges are only a few inches high, in the parterre style. Planted in *Buxus sempervirens* (more commonly known as Box), and measuring only 9.5 metres (31 feet) square, it was designed in the 1980s by Lady Salisbury as part of her attempt to recreate a Tudor garden in front of the Old Palace. The ambience of this low green maze with light gravel paths is most effective, with the red brick tower of the Old Palace providing a vertical element of contrasting colour and texture.

The popular misconception that mazes are usually made of Box probably arises from the rectangular clipped shapes of many hedge mazes, which appear to be box-shaped. Box is an unsuitable material at full human height for a puzzling hedge maze, since it does not hold its shape well at that size, and its stems easily snap. However, at this low height Box is excellent, easy to form and wonderfully coloured.

This is one of two interesting mazes at Hatfield House, the other being closed to the public in the private gardens. It is a tall yew hedge maze, planted in 1840 and designed by Lord Mahon, and thought to replace an even earlier one in the private gardens. Its design is ingenious, in that visitors have to make one and a half spirals around to reach the central goal, and then a reciprocating one and a half spirals to exit at the opposite end of the maze. Its rigorous formality with parallel and right-angled paths and hedges conceals this grand deception.

Though planted in the 1980s, this maze carefully recalls the decorative Tudor mazes, to add an air of authenticity to this recreation of a historical garden. It is designed to be viewed from the surrounding pathways.

HAMPTON COURT PALACE MAZE
SURREY, ENGLAND

The hedge maze at Hampton Court Palace is probably the most famous in the world, as well as one of the earliest to have survived. It was planted as part of the gardens laid out by George London and Henry Wise for King William of Orange between 1689 and 1695. The king clearly had a passion for hedge mazes, since he had already had one created in 1682 at his royal palace at Het Loo in Holland.

The unusual trapezoid shape of the maze at Hampton Court is explained by the plan of the surrounding gardens, known as the 'Wilderness', with its shape dictated by two diagonal paths and a further curving path. Most significantly, it has various junctions and dead ends, so it remains the world's oldest surviving example of a genuine puzzle maze, rather than a labyrinth.

Unquestionably the survival of this maze is due to its location in a royal palace. In fact, the maze faced its gravest threat very early on in its life, when Capability Brown became the Royal Gardener, and for twenty years lived in the house alongside the maze. Brown's reputation had been established by sweeping away some two hundred fine gardens all over the country, but the King expressly ordered Brown not to interfere with the maze.

The Hampton Court Maze was described in Jerome K. Jerome's *Three Men in a Boat*, and this novel established in many minds the connection between mazes, blazers and straw boater hats. Such was its reputation that since Victorian times others have been keen to emulate it when creating hedge mazes elsewhere, and the design has been copied over a dozen times in Britain, North America and Australia. Over three hundred years on from when it was first laid out, today it attracts hundreds of thousands of visitors each year.

VERTICAL MAZES

This distinctive trapezoid plan at Hampton Court was dictated by the unusual angles of the paths in the Wilderness adjacent to the Palace. The design has been widely emulated and copied around the world, sometimes even retaining the asymmetrical angles .

CHATSWORTH HOUSE MAZE
DERBYSHIRE, ENGLAND

The Chatsworth maze has one of the most magnificent settings of any hedge maze anywhere in the world. Chatsworth House, alongside Blenheim (see pp. 46–7), ranks among the very finest homes in Britain, with extensive grounds. The maze itself occupies the former site of Joseph Paxton's 'Great Stove' glasshouse (Paxton later went on to create the famous 'Crystal Palace' for London's Great Exhibition of 1851).

At Chatsworth, the strong brick and stone foundations of the glasshouse still remain in place, covering such a large area that the hedge maze, which is 40 by 35 metres (130 by 115 feet), occupies only the central part, with extensive gardens at each end. The maze, which is planted in yew, is surrounded by mature Wellingtonias, raised grass banks and paths on all sides, and stone bridges at each end. It acts like a 'magnet' in the landscape, drawing visitors through various parts of the Chatsworth gardens.

Although the current maze was planted in 1962, it uses an earlier design of unknown origin. The design is unusual in having several entrances, not all of which actually lead to the central goal – rather than having a single entrance and many internal junctions. Its rectangular shape gives way to a series of concentric rings towards the centre, reinforcing the impression that one has to keep pressing inwards to solve the puzzle. Deceptively, in one place one has to turn outwards towards less tightly curved paths and away from the centre, in order to follow the true path and reach the goal.

The immaculately kept maze at Chatsworth is made from over a thousand yew trees, all very carefully clipped, while at the centre is a weeping pear tree. As the plan above shows, there are four entrances, but only two take you to the centre.

MARLBOROUGH MAZE BLENHEIM PALACE
OXFORDSHIRE, ENGLAND

The Marlborough Maze, situated within the grounds of Blenheim Palace, is a homage to the original inhabitant of the Palace, the First Duke of Marlborough, who was given the Palace in recognition of his victories in the Wars of Spanish Succession. Designed with Randoll Coate in 1991, the elaborate and complex layout is based on the Grinling Gibbons sculpture 'Panoply of Victory' on the roof of the Palace. Seen from above, the yew hedges portray pyramids of cannonballs, a cannon firing, the air filled with banners and flags, and the sound of trumpets. The maze has two brick and stone pavilions set within the high walls to define and reinforce its central axis. The two wooden bridges create a three-dimensional puzzle, as well as giving tantalizing views across parts of the world's largest symbolic hedge maze (measuring 90 by 56 metres, or 294 x 185 feet).

However, the Marlborough Maze was not the first maze in Woodstock Park, where Blenheim is located. Hundreds of years before it had supposedly been the the site of one of history's most colourful and tragic mazes: 'Rosamund's Bower'. The exact site of the fabled Bower is now marked by a well and fountain. 'Fair Rosamund', daughter of Walter de Clifford, was mistress to King Henry II (1133–89), and Henry built this elaborate structure to conceal Rosamund from his queen, Eleanor of Aquitaine. It would have been a most elaborate architectural maze, with solid walls, stout doors, and other physical defences to provide a haven for their illicit liaisons. Finally, in about 1176, Queen Eleanor managed to penetrate the maze, and confronted Rosamund with the choice of a dagger or poisoned chalice. Rosamund chose the poison and died, and it is said that King Henry never smiled again.

LEEDS CASTLE MAZE
MAIDSTONE, KENT, ENGLAND

Set on two Kentish lake islands, Leeds Castle has been described as 'the loveliest castle in the world'. There has been a castle on the site since the ninth century; Queen Eleanor, wife of Edward I, was the first of several Queens of England to live there. In 1974 Lady Baillie, the last private owner, set up a charitable trust to maintain the castle for the nation and for the enjoyment of all, to assist medicine, and to encourage the arts.

The formal hedge maze, opened on 25 May, 1988 by Princess Alexandra, tempts visitors beyond the Culpeper Gardens and the Aviary. The maze is a topiary castle with castellated yew hedges, an entrance bridge and a central tower. From its central raised goal, the view from the stone parapet rewards the visitor with images of a Queen's crown and a chalice, both laid out in the rows of the hedges. Looking down, visitors see splashing water and light

six metres (twenty feet) below them. Beneath the stone tower, they discover the entrance to an underground grotto decorated with thousands of sea shells, with statues in niches, and water cascading over a grotesque face in the manner of the Bomarzo giants in Italy (see p. 50). Still deeper, a 27-metre (90-foot) underground passage beneath the hedges of the maze leads through a dramatic vortex, confronting visitors with a flooded cave, the seat of the nymph of the grotto, before they ascend to the outside world.

In almost any other maze, after reaching the centre visitors would have to retrace their way back on the level, since topologically if the goal is on an island, there cannot be any quick exit path. Nor is there any visible exit bridge. What is out of sight is the maze's underground exit tunnel – a wonderful maze deception! This was the world's first hedge maze open to the public to have such an exit tunnel.

This maze is challenging and teasing in several ways. If visitors try to solve it using the 'hand-on-wall' method, they will travel around the perimeter and return to the entrance. Just one hedgerow from the centre, they can even travel what feels like almost a full circle around a circular path, and yet never find a way in. Gradually they discover that the internal blocks of hedges form several 'islands' – several small ones, and one gigantic island that includes the central goal. The final approach path snakes and turns between other hedges. Underneath the maze is a grotto (above) which the visitor descends into in order to exit. The image opposite shows the maze soon after planting.

A MAZE ING FACTS
How big is it? 2,264 sq. metres
(24,336 sq. feet)
How long are the paths? 935 m. (3,087 ft)
When did it open? 1988
What's it made of? Yew
Did you know? This was the world's first hedge maze with an underground tunnel

MURRAY MAZE SCONE PALACE
SCONE, SCOTLAND

The Murray Maze at Scone Palace in Scotland lies in a majestic and regal setting. Scone Palace has been the place of coronation of Scottish Kings and Queens for centuries. After the kingdoms of England and Scotland were joined to form the United Kingdom, the coronation throne within Westminster Abbey was modified to accommodate the famous Stone of Scone beneath its wooden seat.

However, it's a very playful place as well. An unusual feature of the landscape at Scone is its man-made Moot Hill, also sometimes known as Boot Hill, said to have been built from bootfuls of earth brought by Scottish Chieftains in homage to their king. Just near this hill is the charmingly named Monk's Playgreen, where, until the sacking of the Abbey of Scone in 1559, the monks played their own version of football. Appropriately, this was chosen as the site for the Murray Maze.

The Earl of Mansfield's son Viscount Stormont suggested that the family's heraldic device of the five-pointed Murray Star should be its leitmotiv, which I rashly agreed to, before confronting the realities of the design process. The challenge when designing a maze in the shape of a five-pointed star is how to create a truly puzzling network, when there are five places where the numbers of alleyways are severely limited. Finally inspiration struck and the entire maze was constructed using curves. In addition, a tartan pattern was created using intersecting lines of green beech and copper beech to weave the design. Since the Earl of Mansfield was a patron of the Fountain Society, the goal provided the opportunity for a central fountain, featuring a specially commissioned statue by David William-Ellis, while a splendid Gothic bridge, designed by Vernon Gibberd, provides a quick exit.

©1990, Minotaur Designs
22 May 1990

LABERINT D'HORTA MAZE
BARCELONA, SPAIN

This, the most splendid hedge maze in Spain, was designed in 1791 by Domenico Bagutti for the Marquis of Alfarràs. The maze is situated in the Laberint d'Horta park in the Horta-Guinardó district in Barcelona. The gardens lie on a rising hillside, and there are fine views down onto the maze from stone staircases, balustraded terraces and pavilions higher up the slope. The park's large upper pool is not just for ornament, since ingeniously it also provides a large volume of water and a head of pressure to keep the gardens irrigated throughout the year.

The central goal of the maze is a statue of Eros surrounded by a circle of eight tall arches of clipped cypress. These arches, rising above the tops of the hedges, are an ingenious device to deceive visitors who may be able to view the maze from a high vantage point, as is the situation here. Similar tall arches were used in the 1840s to obscure the design of the hedge maze in Bridge End Gardens in Saffron Walden, England, where raised viewing platforms would otherwise have made it easier to solve the puzzle.

The entire park, which is the oldest extant garden in Barcelona, passed into the hands of the city council in the early 1970s, and since has been steadily restored to its original glory, full of intriguing details and fascinating surprises. More than a century later, between 1900 and 1912, the celebrated Catalan artist Antoni Gaudí created the Parc Güell a few miles across Barcelona, where his work displays the same playful spirit of visual deceptions, jokes and surprises.

This elegant, Neo-Classical maze feels more Italian than Spanish, due to its creator being from that country. At the centre is a statue of Eros, perhaps appropriately, since the gardens are famous for their romantic atmosphere. Rather than yew, as commonly found in northern Europe, this maze is made from local cypresses.

LONGLEAT HEDGE MAZE
WILTSHIRE, ENGLAND

In 1974, the present Lord Bath wanted to create a maze on a scale in keeping with the famous Elizabethan house at Longleat; the result was the world's largest hedge maze. Its paths total 3,084 metres (10,125 feet) in length, and it occupies an area of 6,169 square metres (66,403 square feet).

Opened in 1978, this was one of the first new hedge mazes in Britain for half a century, and set the standard for dozens more in the next quarter century. The maze was designed by Greg Bright, and includes various innovative puzzle features. Six bridges create a three-dimensional puzzle. Spiral junctions are intended to add confusion by repetition. Elongated fork junctions are cunningly used, since visitors are thought to prefer to 'conserve their momentum' instead of making U-turns. The whirling lines and the lack of any grid add further disorientation. The goal is a magnificent tower.

With such lengthy paths, visitors need more than an hour to solve the puzzle and reach the goal. Yet surprisingly for such a large maze there is no quick exit, so visitors make their escape through the same vast network of paths – meaning that the round trip can take up to two hours! Over the years, the Longleat Hedge Maze has gained a cult following, and with the advent of mobile phones, bewildered visitors began to call the Estate Office for guidance so often that a Maze Help Line was installed.

Buoyed up by the project's success, Lord Bath went on to build up a unique collection of mazes at Longleat – the Sun Maze and Moon Labyrinth (both by Randoll Coate), King Arthur's Mirror Maze (see pp. 168–71) and the Labyrinth of Love (by Graham Burgess), as well as a Blue Peter Maze designed by the winner of a competition held by this popular British children's television programme.

The hedge maze at Longleat was for a while the largest in the world. The plan, right, shows, its great complexity There is only one entrance – at the bottom of the plan. Bridges were used to add an extra dimension of complexity, allowing the maze paths to cross over each other and make it even more puzzling.

The maze design is very ingenious, because the first quarter of the maze is like a 'frying pan'; you enter at its 'handle', and whether you keep to the left-hand wall or the right-hand wall, you will always come back to the handle. The only way forward is to find a path that starts in the middle of the frying pan that takes you by bridge over its 'rim'. Several great spiralling patterns confuse further, and if you want to go north, you may need to take the spiral path that starts off heading east and then goes clockwise.

AMAZEING FACTS

How big is it? 6,169 sq. metres (66,403 sq. feet)

How long are the paths? 3,084 m (10,125 ft)

When did it open? 1978

What's it made of? Yew

Did you know? The vast quantity of clippings from this enormous hedge maze are used to produce Taxol, used in the treatment of cancer.

SOMERLEYTON MAZE
NR LOWESTOFT, SUFFOLK, ENGLAND

The Somerleyton Maze was designed and laid out in 1846 by William Nesfield. Its charm arises from the generous scale on which it was laid out, and its delightful pavilion, in the form of a pagoda on a large central raised mound. The design was copied at another of the family's homes, Worden Park in Lancashire, in 1886. In the 1980s, the hedges had become so overgrown that the path was almost impenetrable. The remedy was drastic. First one side of each hedge was cut back to the trunk, and given three years to resprout; then the other side of each hedge was pruned back in the same way. After six years, the maze had fully resprouted and had vibrant narrow hedges, just two feet wide, yet with the thick original trunks of 1846. Yew hedges are very enduring, and can be maintained for centuries.

DARWIN MAZE
EDINBURGH ZOO, SCOTLAND

The Darwin Maze at Edinburgh Zoo was conceived as an experiential interpretation of Darwin's Theory of Evolution – appropriately, it is in the shape of a giant tortoise of the Galapagos Islands. As visitors walk through the maze, they encounter the conditions required for evolution: two genders, predators, natural selection, distinct breeding groups, and the origin of new species. The interpretation of the subject with interactive features is both informative and amusing. For example, in the Chamber of Natural Selection, progress is blocked by rows of foaming fountains that only allow you to pass if you are wearing dark colours – life is cruel! The goal contains a pavement maze portraying an Orang-Utan (see p. 208), while a raised bridge takes visitors out of the Darwin Maze and along a 30 metre (100 foot) border terrace in colourful brick paving portraying the DNA double-helix spiral.

HEVER CASTLE HEDGE MAZE
KENT, ENGLAND

Hever Castle, which dates back to the thirteenth century, has had a colourful history. Between 1462 and 1538 it was the home of the Boleyns, causing Henry VIII to visit while he was courting his future wife, Anne. Centuries later, in 1903, it was acquired by William Waldorf Astor, the American millionaire. In his grand scheme, he added a 'Tudor' village and a unique Italian garden to accommodate his extensive collection of statuary and antiquities. The yew maze and a set of topiary chessmen were laid out between the two moats to recreate a Tudor atmosphere. The combination of moats, yew hedges, and a classic medieval castle makes Hever Castle a most sensational period landscape.

Just as with the maze at Chatsworth, this design attempts the geometric paradox of fitting a circle elegantly within a square; neither succeeds in eliminating awkward triangular cells in the four corners. This design challenge was finally overcome in the Leeds Castle maze (see pp. 48–51), where perpendicular hedges radiate from the centre.

ESCOT PARK HEDGE MAZE
NR HONITON, DEVON, ENGLAND

Situated in beautiful countryside near Honiton, Devon, deep in the English West Country, Escot House and its estate of 1,200 acres has been home to the same family for six generations, since 1794. Several of the buildings are Grade I listed, and there is a continuous challenge to maintain the estate, and ensure it has a relevant role and a sustainable future.

The Escot Maze is the largest single element of a varied range of puzzles, 'Six-Minute' mazes and challenges in the landscape, to attract visitors and achieve estate diversification. The hedge maze itself, which was opened in 2004, has a delightfully abstract five-fold design. It is aligned on the central axis of the walled garden, and draws visitors through two brick arches the full length of the gardens like a magnet in the landscape. The maze design is deceptively simple, being a square 53 metres (175 feet) in each direction; at the centre is a tower with a

jauntily angled roof. However, the maze also contains five bridges tangential to the centre, each advancing 72 degrees with rotational symmetry. Due to the rotational angle, these bridges offer only limted help in orientation and locating the centre. Some of the junctions are marked with wrought-iron arbours with fragrant climbing plants, again adding a little variety and, eventually, welcome shade and texture. Finally, four adjustable and lockable 'Maze Gates' allow the maze to be set in different puzzle configurations, meaning that the layout can be altered from season to season, year to year, to ensure that there are always fresh challenges!

The image opposite shows the maze in its early stages – eventually the hedges should be 1.8 metres (6 feet) high. Here at Escot Park, the beech hedges will achieve their full height within three years; if yew were used it would take between six and eight.

DREAM OF POLIPHILO HEDGE MAZE
CHÂTEAU DE THOIRY, YVELINES, FRANCE

The Château de Thoiry is a fascinating example of Renaissance architecture, the building laden with solar symbolism and meaning – hence its alternative name of 'Le Château du Soleil'. When it was decided to build a maze in the grounds, to go with the existing safari park and a number of other attractions, it therefore seemed natural enough to incorporate this symbolism into the design. The owner, the Viscount de la Panousse (pictured above), was also keen to celebrate the important Renaissance publication the *Hypnerotomachia Poliphili*, which had been written in 1499. This seemed fitting for a maze design since the protagonist of the story gets lost in a wilderness, before having a mystical vision. The dimensions of the maze were to be 110 by 55 metres (360 x 180 feet).

Designing on such a scale required considerable planning, and maze took many years to come to fruition. The final layout, however, reconciles many different themes. The general scheme is of a giant eye; in addition, there are four creatures (bird, fish, owl and lizard), which represent the members of the family who lived in the château. The two elephants with obelisks are taken from the vivid imagery of the *Hypnerotomachia Poliphili* (as well as referring to the elephants kept in the safari park – see above!), while towards the end of the journey visitors encounter three doorways, just as does Poliphilo in the story.

Just as with the maze at Longleat, bridges are used to introduce a three-dimensional element, to orientate, confuse and reward the visitors, though in this case there are no fewer than nine. The five central bridges represent the Five Senses, again a theme taken from the *Hypnerotomachia*.

With its nine bridges, the Thoiry hedge maze has a three-dimensional network of paths that is unparalleled in any other hedge maze. Their various angles help visitors enjoy the views across the maze, and of people on other bridges. Although seemingly laid out at random, the five central bridges share precise five-fold rotational symmetry, a design device that later also appeared in the Escot Park hedge maze (see pp. 66–7). The bridge opposite forms a dramatic entrance to the maze.

DOBBIES MAZE WORLD
ATHERSTONE, WARWICKSHIRE, ENGLAND

Dobbies is a chain of garden centres in the UK which offer entertainment and education alongside their standard range of products. To this end, they have created wildlife wetlands areas with their own interpretation centres, and, at their Atherstone site, 'Maze World'.

Opened in 2004, Maze World has seven mazes which are a celebration of the continents of the world, on an epic scale with a combined total of 3,926 metres (2.44 miles) of paths, covering 7,319 square metres (78,680 square feet). The design captures the character of each continent, yet ensures that together they have a strong collective identity.

The mazes are constructed from a range of materials: some are panel mazes (discussed on pp. 108–111), another is a maize maze, and two of them are hedge mazes. The first of these, representing North America, is the Canadian Hedge Maze, in the shape of a maple leaf. Europe, meanwhile, is represented by a traditional English Garden Hedge Maze (shown opposite) – a perfect square of formal hedges and paths, containing rose arbours, trellis arches, bridges, seating and water features.

This hedge maze, representing North America, takes the form of a Canadian maple leaf. To add to the puzzlement, there are four paved areas with directional arrows within the coloured brickwork, which indicate permitted directions to follow. Visitors who make it to the central goal are rewarded by a real full-size native Indian tepee.

Below is the English Garden Maze, reflecting many of the qualities of traditional hedge mazes, but with additional features for extra interest. Left, meanwhile, is the maze created at Dobbies Garden Centre in Stirling, Scotland. It was inspired by a diagonal Celtic knot pattern of the type found in illuminated manuscripts of the early Middle Ages, and which lend themselves to this sort of right-angled design.

ALICE IN WONDERLAND MAZE
CHRISTCHURCH, DORSET, ENGLAND

This intriguing hedge maze takes as its theme *Alice's Adventures in Wonderland*, the classic children's story written by Lewis Carroll and first published in 1865. In this marvellous book a young girl named Alice falls asleep and finds herself lost in a magical, dream-like land populated with peculiar characters and creatures.

The maze, which measures 73 x 73 metres (240 x 240 feet), is planted with beech and features a wooden bridge and a central mound; it opened in 1991 as the centrepiece of a new seven-acre garden, set amid avenues of topiary and entered under a viewing bridge. The symbolism of the story can be found ingeniously woven into the gigantic shapes formed by the hedges. In this topsy-turvy dream world, none of the images are the same way up, but they are all the right way up when seen from the top of the central mound. Rotating clockwise,

the principal characters in the story are portrayed – Alice, Mad Hatter, White Rabbit, Cheshire Cat, Queen of Hearts, Gryffon, Mock Turtle and Dodo. The centre of the maze portrays the White Rabbit's pocket watch, with steps up and down the mound indicating four o'clock – perpetual tea-time. The central octagon is also the body of a giant teapot, with the Dormouse sleeping in its handle. Finally visitors leave the maze via a short exit, just like the ending of Alice's dream, in a flurry of playing cards.

VERTICAL MAZES

This octagonal maze is one of the world's largest hedge mazes. All eight images within the hedge design are the right way up when seen from the centre. The steps up the central mound are in the positions of the hands of a clock when it is 4pm. The hedges surrounding it are in the shape of a giant teapot.

VILLA PISANI MAZE
STRA, ITALY

This is perhaps the most distinctive hedge maze
in the whole of Italy, as well as one of the oldest,
dating to 1720. It is made particularly impressive
by the magnificent stone tower at its centre.
This broad tower has twin external spiral
staircases, which allows visitors to ascend
and descend simultaneously at busy times.
The staircases with their delightfully
decorative handrails give access to
doorways set at different levels facing
outwards. A statue of Minerva completes
the top of the tower.

BAMBOO LABYRINTH
ALNWICK GARDEN
NORTHUMBERLAND
ENGLAND

The Alnwick Garden, in the grounds of Alnwick Castle, opened in October 2002, and is one of the most exciting gardens of the past century. Created by the Duchess of Northumberland as a 12-acre public space accessible to all, it features spectacular water displays, a 'Poison' garden, and one of the largest tree houses in the world.

The Bamboo Labyrinth was made from a new Chinese variety of bamboo, *'Fargesia' rufa*, planted on waist-high banks. Distinctive clay brick paving depicting its paths as streams, and these paths also contain bronze leaves, scattered at random to look as if they have been blown down from the bamboo. At the centre is a circular carved stone that reveals the maze design so that you can solve it again.

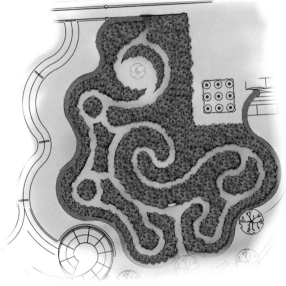

DRAGON MAZE
NEWQUAY ZOO, CORNWALL, ENGLAND

Mythical creatures have been associated with mazes ever since the Cretan Labyrinth which was inhabited by a Minotaur, half man and half bull. And what better place to find a mythical creature, than in a zoo? At Newquay Zoo, in Cornwall, the very irregularity of the available plot, which measures 64 x 26 metres (210 by 85 feet), lent itself to a dragon design, with the energy of its fiery mouth, hungry eyes, claws, wings and barbed tail coiled up ready to spring into action.

Dragons are one of the most widespread mythical creatures in Britain. Ancient ley lines, or 'dragon lines', run as straight as eyesight for miles criss-crossing the English countryside, joining up hilltops, standing stones, wells and sacred places. Dragons appear in medieval heraldry, as well as in Christian traditions such as those of St George and St Michael. Cornwall's most notable island is known as St Michael's Mount, matching its French counterpart Mont Saint Michel across the English Channel.

Mythical creatures are often feared within labyrinths, but here the beast is the labyrinth itself. One can imagine this menacing creature occupying the nearby St Michael's Mount until the advent of Christianity, when life got too hot for dragons. Whatever his misty past, the zoo keepers have at last found him a safe paddock all to himself. Since this is Cornwall, he enjoys the protection of the Duke of Cornwall, the Heir Apparent, and so wears about his neck the heraldic collar of the Eldest Son, which is a label of three points. The hedges are Eleagnus, and the maze was designed with Randoll Coate in 1984.

The Jasmine Maze in China was commissioned as the world's largest maze, and was planted in the summer of 2003. Because of its great size, it seemed exciting to portray the Universe, with sun, moon, stars and planets. The 22,263 square metre (240,000 square foot) design boasts eight kilometres (five miles) of pathway and fourteen bridges. Since opening is being timed to coincide with the 2008 Olympics, there are three levels of difficulty, with bronze, silver and gold routes.

JASMINE MAZE
YUNNAN PROVINCE, CHINA

WILLIAMSBURG HEDGE MAZE
VIRGINIA, USA

America's most famous hedge maze is in the gardens of the Governor's Palace at Colonial Williamsburg, Virginia. The town of Williamsburg is a 'living history' recreation of America's colonial past, complete with costumed actors. While there was no hedge maze in Williamsburg's true colonial past, its inclusion in the gardens feels appropriate, with its planting date of 1935 steadily receding beyond living memory. The maze measures 29 by 27 metres (95 by 88 feet) – about half the size of the Hampton Court maze upon whose design it is based.

GOLDEN JUBILEE MAZE
STAUNTON COUNTRY PARK, HAMPSHIRE, ENGLAND

Staunton was originally the Regency pleasure gardens and parkland created by the politician and botanist, Sir George Staunton. He funded plant collectors, and helped Britain establish a worldwide reputation for botanical collections. Several plants still bear Sir George's name today.

The park passed into public ownership, and became Staunton Country Park. The Golden Jubilee Maze and Puzzle Garden, opened in 2002, was a celebration of fifty years of the reign of Queen Elizabeth II. The Puzzle Garden has curling paths, in the manner of curving rose stems. They lead visitors to various horizontal, vertical, two-dimensional and three-dimensional puzzles and 'Six Minute' mazes, surrounded by raised banks with extensive shrub and floral planting.

The yew hedge maze has a delightful design of a central octagon, with six indentations and further paths that extend 22 by 18 metres (73 by 59 feet) to form a rectangle. Five wrought-iron arbours, with curling metal spirals, support honeysuckle and different types of climbing roses grown by Sir George Staunton. The central eight-pillared arbour is surmounted by a golden royal crown, again to celebrate the Golden Jubilee. Under each of the other four arbours is an area of decorative paving with arrows that dictate the directions in which the visitor can continue, imposing rules and making the maze puzzle trickier.

Two colourful and brightly painted Speaking Tubes allow younger visitors to talk to each other across the maze, and two wrought-iron gates within the maze use the heraldic images of the Queen's royal beasts, the Lion and the Unicorn. Each of these Maze Gates is a puzzle in its own right, since each contains a maze pattern that can be solved by finger or by eye.

AMAZEING FACTS

How big is it? 396 sq. metres
(4,300 sq. feet)

When did it open? 2002

What's it made of? Yew

Did you know? The five arbours represent
the five decades of the rule of Queen
Elizabeth II.

RUSSBOROUGH MAZE CO. WICKLOW, IRELAND

Russborough House in Co. Wicklow is the finest example of a grand 18th-century house in Ireland, and makes the perfect setting for this delightful puzzle maze. The house is approached along an impressive avenue of mature beech trees, and this gave us confidence to plant the hedge maze in beech. The family who commissioned the maze had been early pioneers in the South African diamond industry. They wanted a hedge maze without symbolism, but with straight lines and right angles. However, the final design, planted in 1989, includes a series of diamonds at the centre. A statue of Cupid, atop a tall column, indicates the central goal.

DOLPHINS MAZE MONIGA DEL GARDA, ITALY

The Dophins Maze lies on the western shore of Lake Garda in Italy, and was inspired by the true story of the 'Boy and the Dolphin' which was recorded in Classical Roman times. Two gigantic dolphins chase each other round in circles in an endless pursuit. The owner wanted the maze to be able to offer a different puzzle to visitors on successive days of their holidays, and so there are seven moveable gates, which can be set in different positions to provide completely different puzzle challenges. A Victory Bridge allows visitors to reach a quick exit.

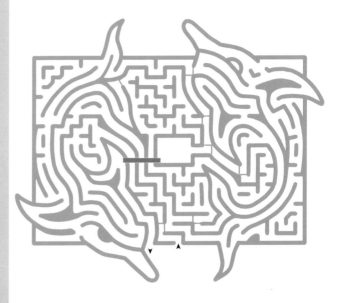

COMICAL FACE
MEXICO

Based on a Japanese character, this takes the form
of a giant, comical face. Visitors begin at the
bottom (the chin), choosing the left or right paths,
before snaking along the contours of the head, past
the ears and swirling eyes (though if you get as far
as the top knot you've probably gone wrong!),
along the way stopping to enjoy displays of flowers.
The goal is the gaping mouth, from where there is
a quick exit. Three bridges, which offer panoramic
views across the maze, and a number of adjustable
gates, ensure that there is ample variety.

THROOP MAZE
BOURNEMOUTH, DORSET

This was my very first maze, created at Throop
House. It was planned for a site overshadowed by
ancient oak woodland where little would grow
except holly. The positions of the trees and clumps
of holly were plotted, and a site plan was produced.
The long holly stems were then bent over and held
down to form new roots in the shape of the maze.
The design can be solved by a 'Logic Lance', by
consistently turning Left-Right-Left-Right.

NEW HARMONY MAZE
INDIANA, USA

Neither private nor public mazes seem to have been very popular in the early history of the United States. An exception, however, is this maze that was planted in Indiana by a community of German immigrants who called themselves the Harmony Society. This group, which arrived in America in 1803–4, was a Protestant sect led by its founder George Rapp. While European garden mazes at this time were becoming largely decorative amusements, the Rappites' maze had great symbolic purpose, being intended to symbolize the spirit of their movement and the work needed to achieve true harmony.

The original maze at New Harmony, as planted in *c*. 1815, was formed from vines and shrubs. This fell into disrepair in the mid-nineteenth century, and was largely forgotten until it was restored between 1939 and 1941. At the centre was a peculiar structure, roughly clad, and with a secret, hidden entrance.

Once inside, however, visitors would be stunned by an ornate, richly decorated interior, recalling a Greek temple (the walls of the reconstruction also feature a selection of Rapp's proverbs). As with so many of the Utopian communities of the nineteenth century, within a few years it had fallen apart amid internal dissent and financial problems.

Although it looks deceptively like a simple unicursal labyrinth, it is not. Visitors can choose any one of three paths to enter the maze. Some choices will lead to dead ends (there are two tantalizingly close to the centre), or even the surrounding lawns, while there is an extra trap for those trying to leave the centre.

SEAHORSE MAZE
PARC MELI, BELGIUM

Parc Meli is a theme park in Belgium that grew out of a honey business. This charming and engaging maze, which opened in 1997, was designed for the aquatic themed area. In recent years it has become very popular to give mazes symbolic or intricate shapes, in this case a seahorse, one of the most mysterious and magical of maritime creatures.

Visitors try to find their way through the swirling contours of the form, beginning at the tail, and ending at the mouth (where a fountain marks the eye). To make it a little easier, there are a number of paths through, though there are still enough distractions and infuriatingly long dead ends to confound any overconfident visitor!

THE LABYRINTH OF LOVE CHÂTEAU DU COLOMBIER, FRANCE

This maze, some sixty metres (200 feet) square, was commissioned by the same couple who built the maze at Château de Thoiry (see p. 69), and just as at Thoiry there is a strong symbolical element. Since it was set in the grounds of a medieval château, it was decided that the maze should celebrate 'courtly love'. Visitors enter through a parting waterfall, while the patterns of the hedges represent five attributes of courtly love, and are symbolized in the maze design in the form of a peacock for male beauty, the unicorn for purity and maidenly virginity, a knight's helm bearing the colour of his lady's favour, the eternal triangle within a heart denoting the ever-present danger of love betrayed, before finally reaching the central rose of true love.

THE CANADIAN EXPERIENCE MAZE
SAUNDERS FARM,ONTARIO, CANADA

Opened in June 2004, the Canadian Experience
One-Way Maze consists of paths meandering among
great swathes of landscaped rocks, trees and water,
to create the impression of the natural beauty of
Canada, and its flora and fauna,
in miniature.

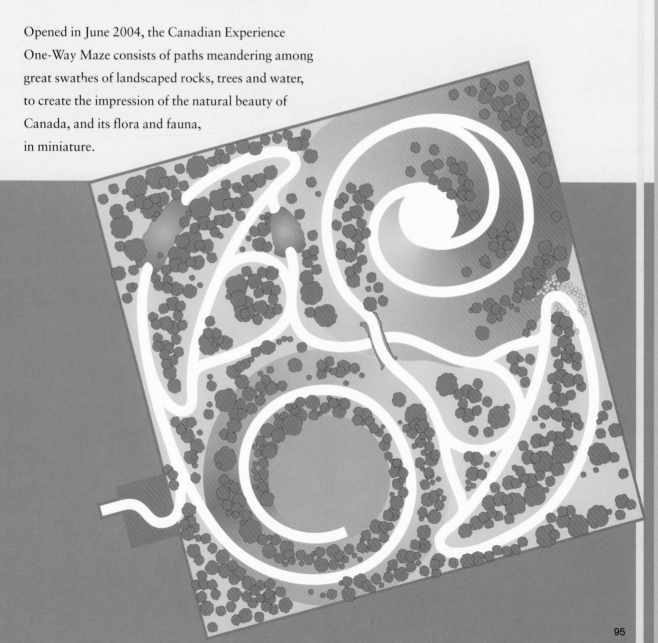

THE CRICKET MAZE
HAMPSHIRE, ENGLAND

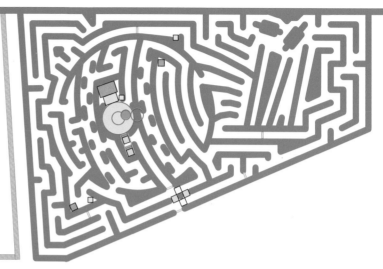

A private maze can sometimes become an extension of one's personal lifestyle. This astonishing and unique willow hedge maze on a private estate in southern England was commissioned to celebrate the owner's passion for cricket, and this most English of games pervades every aspect of the design. The entrance is guarded by a distinctive wrought iron 'cricket' maze gate in brightly coloured metalwork, with bat, ball, stumps, flying bails and white creases. From the sky, the maze paths also portray a game of cricket, with a giant cricket ball bouncing forwards having sent stumps and bails flying. The willow hedges provide a constant reminder of the game's finest sound, the crack of 'leather on willow'.

The end result is a place where the owner can go when he wants to be left undisturbed, perhaps to read a favourite book while sipping a glass of gin and tonic on a warm summer's evening. A good

G&T would need ice, of course, which in turn would require a fridge. So, a small pavilion at the centre of the maze was added to house his fridge – naturally in the style of a cricket pavilion. In front of the pavilion was built a terrace, formed from a circle of decorative Mitre brick paving, portraying his two heraldic dragons, each side of a vertical water feature symbolizing 'the pearl of the East'. This remorseless chain of logic converted splendidly into landscape reality.

THREE LANDS POINT MAZE
NR VALLS, THE NETHERLANDS

Three Lands Point is where the territories of Germany, Belgium and the Netherlands meet, and is the highest point in the Netherlands. The challenge was to create a distinctive maze that would appeal to the million visitors each year that come to this popular beauty spot in the Dutch forests.

The maze design abounds in sets of three, with a three-pointed maze outline containing three heraldic images, three symmetrical bridges, and three foaming fountains in each of its nine (3x3) rows of Foaming Fountain Gates, finally reaching a three-pointed central goal area. The Dutch Lion, German Eagle and Belgian Lion each face their respective countries. In the maze courtyard, a three-fold colour maze combines the flags of the three countries, with the European Flag as its central goal.

Although water features have been used in great gardens since Renaissance times, historically the same has not been true in mazes. This maze was one of the first to introduce water throughout the maze, with close-up water encounters at full body height, provided by the thick sparkling frothy pillars of its 'Foaming Fountain Gates'. The maze bridges already make it a three-dimensional puzzle; with the fountains either blocking the way or allowing people to pass from one minute to another, these create a maze puzzle with a fourth dimension – of time! Once the maze is solved, the central goal contains a lookout tower, with views across the maze and the surrounding countryside beyond. Then there is a Quick Exit path to the Maze Courtyard, with smaller 'Six Minute' mazes to solve.

This is the most popular hedge maze in The Netherlands, a country so keen on puzzles and gardening that it contains over fifty mazes and labyrinths despite its small size.

The bridges within the Three Lands Point
Maze are of a distinctive design, since their top
decks are wider than the flights of steps at each
end. This allows plenty of visitors to linger on the
handrails on each side, admiring the view, without
impeding the progress of those who want to pass
immediately over each bridge.

The laurel maze at Glendurgan, near Falmouth, Cornwall, was created by Alfred Fox in 1833, and is among Britain's earliest surviving hedge mazes. It is one of three mazes today owned by the National Trust (the other two being at Greys Court and Tatton Park). The free-flowing design was a highly innovative departure from formal patterns, as was its positioning on one side of the narrow valley, giving an almost bird's eye view of its sinuous hedges from the other side.

In the 1980s it was discovered that the maze was based at least partly on the famous destroyed eighteenth-century maze at Sydney Gardens, Bath. Because of its newfound importance for maze history, the National Trust agreed to restore it between 1991 and 1994, when the maze was reopened to the public.

GLENDURGAN MAZE
NR FALMOUTH, CORNWALL, ENGLAND

CAPEL MANOR MAZE
MIDDLESEX, ENGLAND

This Italianate maze forms one of a series of period gardens recreated at Capel Manor. It represents the nineteenth-century craze in England for Italianate gardens. During the 1830s and 1840s several Italian-style hedge mazes were planted, including one in Bridge End Gardens at Saffron Walden, and William Nesfield's designs at Somerleyton Hall. This is not a direct copy of any single maze, but rather a synthesis of characteristic elements, including a neat perimeter with semicircular ends.

PANEL MAZES

Quick to set up and easy to maintain, panel mazes offer fast, fun and colourful puzzles that can be created and reconfigured almost anywhere.

Panel fence mazes have two great advantages. They can be built using modular parts in a few weeks, and they are ideal when space is at a premium, since their narrow barriers allow the paths to occupy almost all of the available area – unlike hedge mazes.

Early evidence of the idea of a panel fence maze is an 1893 patent by Ferdinand Guth, 'a subject of the Emperor of Austria, living in New York', for a panel maze made of timber, with revolving doors to change the design, and a viewing platform. Two of the earliest known examples of panel mazes bear remarkable similarities, and appeared on opposite sides of the Atlantic about the turn of the twentieth century; while we cannot directly connect these to Ferdinand Guth, the timing makes it possible. 'The House of Terror' was built at Old Orchard Beach, Maine, USA, about 1900; it was a wooden fence maze using concentric circles, clearly

opposite The panel maze at the Parque Saturno, Barcelona, Spain, late nineteenth/early twentieth century

made of wooden panels, with radial spars for stability, and a central tower with steps. The European example was in Barcelona, Spain, again about 1900, again circular with radial spars, with a thematic doorway in the form of two trees.

Small panel fence mazes, normally on a rectangular grid for simpler construction, became cost-effective features at funfairs and seaside attractions during the early twentieth century, especially in America where timber was widely available and affordable. Although from the outset they had raised platforms as viewing positions, there is no evidence that they exploited the third dimension with bridges to create truly three-dimensional puzzle networks.

Old Orchard Beach panel maze, Maine, USA, early twentieth century

In spite of this early interest, the heyday of panel mazes was between 1984 and 1988 – in Japan. Soon it had more panel mazes than any other country, and these were on a far larger scale than ever before. It all arose from the work of a lone Englishman, Stuart Landsborough, in a remote part of New Zealand at Wanaka, South Island. Two Japanese businessmen visited his wooden panel maze, discussed it with him, and left. The following year they returned, and he had added bridges and a puzzle room; the transformation of bridges and their three-dimensional puzzlement electrified them.

They went back to Japan, and between 1984 and 1988, commissioned Stuart to design over twenty wooden mazes of increasing complexity. In each one, the challenge was to reach four Stations in the corners, and stamp the letters M-A-Z-E on a card in the fastest time. Visitors turned up in running

shoes and shorts; the best daily and weekly names and their times were shown on giant displays. The nation went maze crazy, and at one time there were over 200 wooden panel mazes in Japan. Like all crazes, however, the passion for mazes subsided, and now most of those mazes have made way for even more profitable uses of their land.

Most of the wooden fence mazes in America have been built since the 1980s. Several wooden mazes appear each summer in ski resorts in Colorado, to be taken down each winter to make way for car parking. Permanent wooden panel fence mazes are found in seaside resorts and holiday areas, since they tie in well with related activities such as mini-golf and other informal family pastimes. Those along the gulf coast sometimes suffer from hurricane damage.

Panel Mazes have also been created in Europe, including at Holywell Bay in Cornwall, and at

Dobbies Maze World in Warwickshire. At Bicton
Park in Devon, the wooden fences are for younger
visitors and consist entirely of vertical posts with
a capping rail; another notable example is the
distinctive wooden fence maze at Kelburn, near
Glasgow, Scotland, with its distinctive central
pagoda and levels of varying heights. Perhaps the
most interesting example, however, is the Multi-
Sensory Mobility Maze for the Blind in Worcester,
where various types of wooden fences are used to
add variety as children practise their mobility skills.

A bird's eye view of a typical Japanese wooden panel maze
of the 1980s

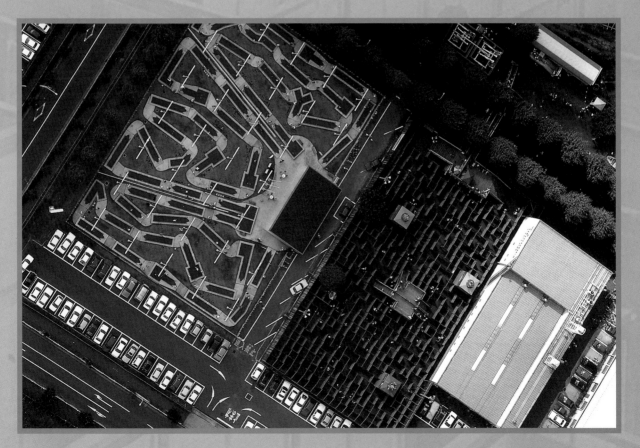

AFRICAN REED FENCE MAZE
DOBBIES MAZE WORLD

Within the Dobbies Maze World complex (see p. 73) the shape of the African Maze interfaces like a jigsaw piece with its neighbouring Japanese and Australian mazes, while at the same time suggesting the head and distinctive horn of the rhino. The reed fences symbolize the tall grasses of the African plains.

The goal is a creative interpretation of modern Africa, with a circular enclosure wall decorated and painted in the distinctive style of the Ndebele people of Southern Africa. A safari Land Rover with zebra camouflage markings symbolizes the sustainable African tourist industry of the future.

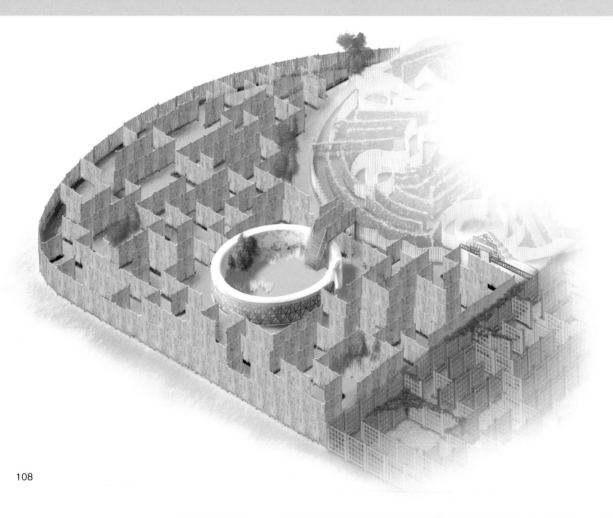

AUSTRALIAN POLE MAZE
DOBBIES MAZE WORLD

The pathway patterns of the Australian maze reflect the sinuous decorated lines of traditional Aboriginal bark paintings. The two different treatments of the wooden pole barriers of varying heights reflect the colours used in Aboriginal paintings. The spiralling barriers created four feature areas for artwork, as well as a large circular central garden, from which a raised bridge provides a quick exit leading to the next Dobbies maze challenge.

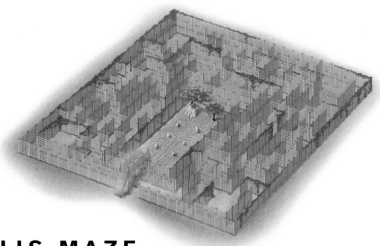

JAPANESE TRELLIS MAZE
DOBBIES MAZE WORLD

The Japanese maze at Dobbies Maze World was intended to achieve a complete change of pace from the emphatically hard maze barriers of the other continents, such as Australia and Africa. The light open trellis walls allow the breeze and sounds to travel through the maze. As the climbing plants gradually grow up using the trellis for support, the character of the maze will evolve into a luxuriant garden of green alleyways, with delicate stems and leaves instead of the more robust foliage of hedging shrubs – a blend of panel and hedge maze.

The goal of the maze is pure delight and a fine reward for reaching it. The entire area is a Japanese garden with water features and characteristic use of bamboo and other materials, yet carried out in a highly contemporary way.

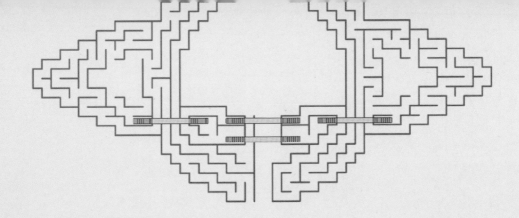

MAZE OF THE PLANETS
EAST TAWAS, MICHIGAN, USA

The gigantic Maze of the Planets, now sadly dismantled, measured 76.2 metres (250 feet) long, and, when seen in plan, portrayed the planet Saturn. Four wooden bridges gave the added impression of its iconic rings passing in front of the planet.

The wooden fencing panels had gaps between each plank, partly to allow visitors to glimpse each other exploring the pathways, and partly to allow strong winds to pass through the structure rather than damage it. Sunlight shining through the gaps created interesting patterns on other fences or on the ground, which changed as the angle of the sun moved throughout the day. Especially on overcast days, when one could not use the sun to orientate oneself, the sheer scale of the maze conspired with the unremitting modular wooden panels to create an experience of mounting confusion. The more one tried to set aside one's sense of disorientation, the more confusing it became.

However, the reward of this maze was well worth the journey – a splendid roofed central tower with twin staircases, one to ascend, and the other to descend, in a manner similar to the central maze tower built in 1720 at Villa Pisani at Stra in Italy. Next to this central tower, in the inner courtyard, was a planet-shaped Colour Maze of plastic tiles to solve (see overleaf), and further 'Six Minute' mazes in the outer courtyard.

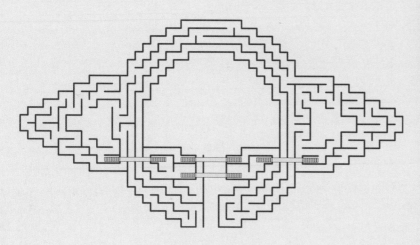

The plan above shows how the bridges form part of the 'rings' around Saturn – a rather fun visual twist. At the goal of the panel maze was a further Colour Maze.

MULTI-SENSORY MOBILITY MAZE
RNIB, WORCESTER, ENGLAND

This, the world's first maze for the blind, was built in 1993 at Britain's premier secondary school of the Royal National Institute for the Blind. This maze provides a safe training environment for blind and partially sighted students to practise moving around in a confusing and dangerous world of bollards and lamp-posts. Accordingly, the maze includes many different textures that are found in the outside world. Students and teachers were consulted in its design, and the mobility teachers consider the final maze provides three years of useful training.

FORT CUSTER MAZE OHIO, USA

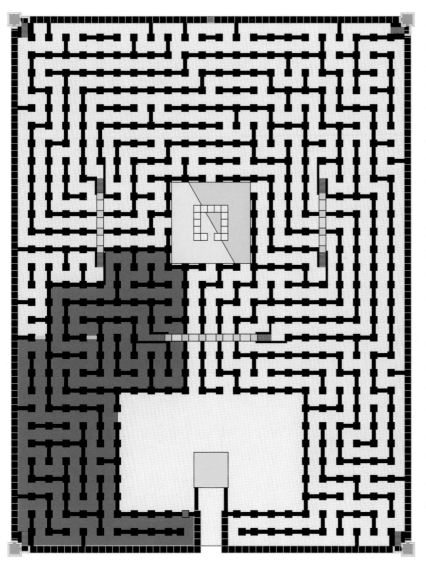

A most unusual wooden maze and a fine example of recycling is the Fort Custer Maze, in Ohio. The family had been in the fruit business for many years, and had accumulated hundreds of wooden crates used for transportation to market. With changes in business patterns, these crates were no longer needed, and it was decided that they would make an excellent module for building a maze. This resulted in a maze of startling complexity and originality. Within General Custer's Fort, one can walk the battlements at high levels, as well as use the various wooden bridges that form an intriguing three-dimensional network of paths.

BICTON PARK FENCE MAZE
DEVON, ENGLAND

Bicton Park in Devon is a fine landscape garden, with an elegant elliptical glasshouse, terraces, lakes and fountains. The wooden fence maze was built in the children's playground in 1986, in the shape of a giant footprint. Measuring a colossal 48 x 23 metres (160 x 75 feet), the owner of the foot to the same scale would be the height of the Eiffel Tower!

The maze is built of vertical wooden posts, at a little lower than adult's shoulder height. At the goal in the heel is a roundabout, while the tall fences also act as a windbreak for a picnic area.

MEDIA INNOVATIONS MAZE MEXICO

This intriguing fence panel maze in the grounds of a science centre in Mexico is less of a maze with a single goal, than an arena for an ingenious puzzle challenge, carried out by interacting with the various electronic panels that are controlled and linked to each other. The design challenge was to fit the maze design around the existing trees without removing any of them, as well as creating overhead bridges and underpass passages that interlink between the various activity areas. The end result is a maze plan that cannot begin to convey the puzzle challenge that awaits its visitors – and each day its electronic puzzle challenge is different! All in all, a fascinating fusion of hi-tech and low-tech.

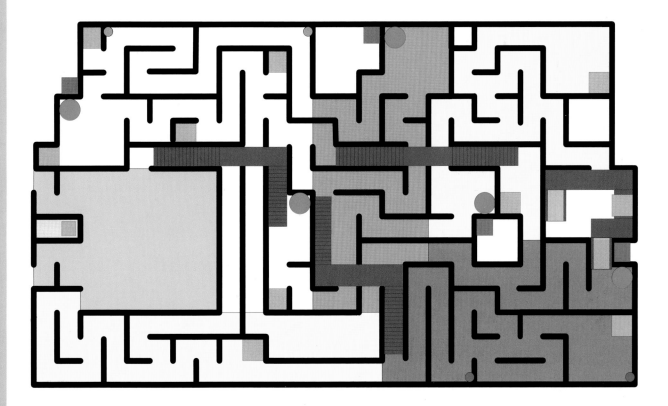

CELTIC AND NAUTICAL MAZES
LEGOLAND, NR WINDSOR, BERKSHIRE, ENGLAND

The design of the Celtic Maze at Legoland is based on the decorative patterns on the famous bronze Battersea Shield, which was found in the tidal mud of the River Thames at Battersea in London.

Visitors enter the Celtic Maze through a passage of vertical stones, reminiscent of ancient burial mounds in the British Isles. The final part is covered by a horizontal stone lintel that forms an archway into the maze. Once inside, the maze recreates the character of a Celtic village, using walls of wattle fencing between vertical posts. The perimeter of the village is defended by a raised mound with a walkway along its ridge, so that defenders can patrol along, looking outwards over this defensive wattle fence. The defensive walkway rises to accommodate the entrance arch.

The goal is a circular thatched meeting house. The only way forward out of this maze is along a tunnel of curved willow, which twists and turns sinuously to the edge of the maze, leading on to the other two Legoland mazes in this trio – the Tudor Hedge Maze, and the Nautical Maze.

The Nautical Maze at Legoland, above, has a circular shape that evokes a ship's compass or wheel. Some of the inner walls are wooden panels, while the outer barriers are made of open trellis, which will eventually be covered by climbing plants. Other panels are made of stretched fabric in various colours, held and tensioned using stainless steel and bronze sailing fittings, with the use of intersecting primary colours capturing the spirit of nautical signalling flags. In places there are portholes within the wooden panels, allowing children to see each other in different pathways. Ships' steering wheels fixed to the panel walls allow everyone to take turns in charge of the ship.

Above is the Celtic Maze, made from wattle, a technique used
to build houses in medieval Europe. The maze conjures up an
Anglo-Saxon community, complete with battlements.

Below is the brightly coloured Nautical Maze at Legoland. At the goal of the maze, there is a gigantic central globe made of brightly coloured pieces of Lego bricks, which rotates to the touch of the hand. Effective navigation brings you safely back to port!

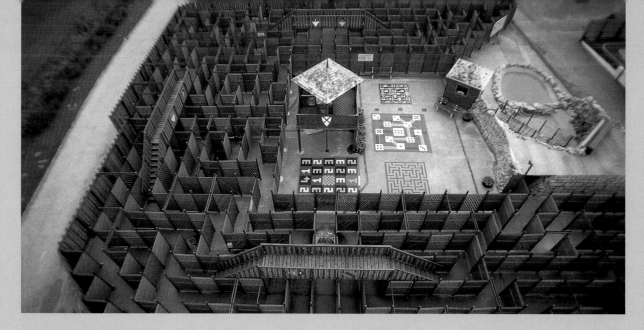

MERLIN'S MAGICAL MAZE
HOLYWELL BAY, CORNWALL, ENGLAND

Holywell Bay Fun Park sits on the top of a high headland, facing the full brunt of Atlantic winter storms. Upon entering, visitors walk towards the pool and its waterfall, which initially is closed and is blocking their way. As they cross the footbridge across the pool, the waterfall magically parts and allows them to enter Merlin's cave without getting wet. Beyond the cave, the maze of wooden fences sets an intriguing challenge, with bridges taking paths over and under each other in a three-dimensional puzzle. Perceptive visitors will notice that some of the panels are in fact maze gates, which the staff unlock and change from day to day, thus ensuring that even if the same holidaymakers visit on consecutive days they will face a new puzzle

challenge. Even during the same visit, the design is also changing from moment to moment, as 'Foaming Fountain Gates' rise and fall within the alleys, blocking the way or allowing progress.

The goal contains a splendid tower approached up a spiral staircase. Its roof is set at 45 degrees to the rest of the tower, thus creating a jaunty image, and also creating in effect four 'balconies' open to the sky looking out over the maze in four directions. From the central tower, visitors can look down on people playing with the various Colour Mazes and other 'Six Minute' mazes in the central courtyard.

MAIZE MAZES

Since the very first maize maze in 1993, the form has become outstandingly popular around the world. The maze may only last for one season – but this means that the designer can come up with something even more difficult the following year!

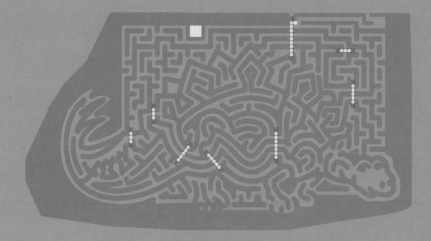

left Stegosaurus Maize Maze, Tulleys Farm, 2004

opposite A family exploring the Pirate Maze at Tulleys Farm in 1999, carrying flags with the skull and crossbones.

Gigantic mazes covering several acres with miles of paths between tall vegetation, existing for just one summer and each year being razed to the ground, might seem beyond the realms of fantasy. Yet by using an agricultural crop, and selecting tough fast-growing maize stalks that grow an inch a day, this suddenly becomes feasible.

Don Frantz, a Broadway theatre producer with Disney, was flying above the maize cornfields of America, saw their maze-like rows of stalks, and started toying with the words 'maze of maize'. It tied in with America's love affair with maize cornfields from the movie *Field of Dreams* onwards. Don spoke with various people, but no one knew how to turn it into a reality. However, when he contacted me in early 1993, I could immediately see how a standalone maize maze attraction would work. Stephen Sondheim suggested the phrase 'Amazing Maize Maze', while Don's theatrical flair and ideas added an extra dimension to the maze experience.

Together Don and I created the world's first maize maze at Lebanon Valley College, Annville, Pennsylvania in 1993. It was the year of the film *Jurassic Park*, so the three-acre maze depicted a Stegosaurus, while its 'Maze Courtyard' included a turf labyrinth and various colour mazes. The result was a maze of impressive pedigree. That year there had been devastating floods across the Midwest inundating thousands of square miles of maize; the idea of using a field of corn as a high profile way of raising funds and awareness for farmers who had lost everything captured the nation's imagination. Over one weekend, we set a new maze record as recognized by the Guinness Book of World Records, attracted 6,000 visitors, and raised $32,000 for the Red Cross flood appeal.

For many years, brothers Edward and Lindsay Heyes at Symonds Yat in England had been giving lively introductory talks to every visitor to their hedge maze, complete with Edwardian blazers and boaters and unicycles. Together Don and I transformed the pep talk into an Adventure Briefing that introduces and explains the various maze challenges.

Don and I set two further maize maze world records, at Shippensburg, Pennsylvania (1995) and at Dearborn, Michigan (1996), each time introducing refinements to the maize maze experience: a flag for each family to carry, quiz trails, activity sheets to fill in and take home, and speaking tubes hundreds of feet through the maze. Instead of one weekend, these mazes were operated for four weeks and more; the feasible maximum is typically eight weeks between the time the crop is adult-height, and the corn stalks turn brown and brittle.

The rapid spread of maize mazes across America and the world arose from various factors coming together – they captured the public imagination, gave good value entertainment, and offered a cost-effective form of farm diversification at a time of falling crop prices. By 2003 there were over 300 maize mazes in America, and another 100 worldwide. In Britain, we set our fourth Guinness World Record at Millets Farm in Oxfordshire with a Windmill Maze in 1996, and fifth and sixth world records at Stewarts Garden Lands in Dorset with a Stag Maze in 2002, and a Lobster Maze in 2003. There are now some 40 maize mazes each year in Britain, and more across Europe.

The pace of innovation has scarcely faltered. Multiple bridges that form puzzling three-dimensional networks have become an annual feature at Tulleys Farm, Millets Farm, Davis Megamaze and Belvedere Plantation. Distinctive Y-shaped and X-shaped bridges add further excitement. Davis Megamaze achieved the world's first double-decker bridge in a corn maze in 2001, and each year since. At each farm, all the bridges have to be taken apart and rebuilt the following year.

The total visitor experience has lengthened to two or three hours or more, and evolved to match to visitors' tastes and expectations. Families sometimes spend longer in the Maze Courtyard than the main maze itself, enjoying a range of 'Six Minute' mazes. Once inside the maize maze, their principal objective of finding the goal is enhanced by solving further quiz trails and challenges, and meeting costumed characters. Paul Swaffield at Rodden Farm in Dorset provides probably the finest Maze Courtyard of all, increasing the average visit time to five or six hours.

Most maize mazes are found on farms, though their diverse locations have included castles, châteaux, stately homes, safari parks, garden centres, a Teddy Bear Factory in Vermont, a botanic garden in Ohio and a cinema in Missouri.

One final point: the words corn and maize are sometimes but not always interchangeable. 'Corn' is the name of the most common crop in each country: in England, therefore, it describes wheat, which only grows to 1 metre (3 feet) in height; in America, 'corn' refers to maize, which can grow 2 to 3 metres (8 to 12 feet) high. Thus in America, mazes of maize are known as Corn Mazes; in England they are called Maize Mazes.

At Tulleys Farm, there is only temporary planning permission for each bridge, so these structures are modular for easy transportation at the end of each summer season. This has the advantage that each year's design can position the bridges differently, thus ensuring a fresh baffling puzzle each year.

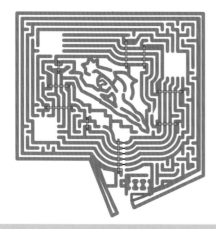
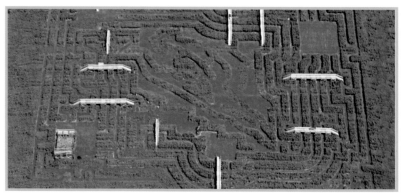

A TALE OF TWO MAZES
DAVIS MEGAMAZE AND TULLEYS FARM

To a large extent the success of a maize maze depends on the energy and commitment of the farmer or owner. The two projects discussed here – one in the United States, the other in England – represent two very different, though equally successful, approaches to maize maze operation and promotion.

The annual Davis Megamaze in Sterling, Massachusetts (see pp. 132–5), is consistently one of the most notable corn mazes in North America, as well as one of the most highly attended, with over 50,000 visitors each summer. Larry Davis had his first maze in 1998, and every year has added innovations, even when it has involved extra labour, cost and ingenuity. In 2001 his maze boasted the world's first double-decker bridge in a cornfield, set within the design of a Tyrannosaurus Rex. Other designs using double-decker bridges have included a Spy's Compass, a Sheriff's Badge and a Royal Crown. There are two dozen design objectives to meet simultaneously, which include fitting the distinctively shaped field, providing areas for interactive Introductory Encounters, a Halfway Goal for refreshments and an optional quick exit over the Victory Bridge; a Final Goal with the same quick exit; and scope for thematic stories and role playing.

In 1999, Davis Megamaze was voted the best new visitor attraction in Massachusetts, and across America it is considered the 'grand-daddy of them all', against which all other corn mazes are compared.

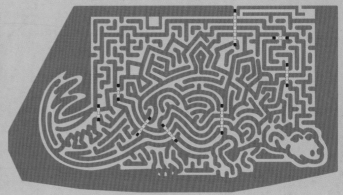

Tulleys Farm in England is a fully functioning retail farm, as well as now being an essential destination for all puzzle enthusiasts. From the first corn maze at Tulleys Farm in 1998, it was clear we would be designing 'outside the box' – in that year literally, since the design of the fantasy dragon appeared to burst outside its rigid rectangular frame. The owner Stuart Beare is an irrepressible fount of creative ideas. One year, visitors were led to believe they had survived an emergency landing in the Amazon jungle; they turned the corner among tall cornstalks and found a complete light aircraft stranded within the field. Within moments, someone in a safari suit emerged, welcomed them, congratulated them on having survived their crash landing unscathed, told them how dangerous the jungle was and then mysteriously melted away among the cornstalks; this is how visitors began to piece together the challenge that had been prepared for them! Another year, the pirate theme culminated at the goal with a complete desert island of many tons of sand, half-buried treasure, and several palm trees growing in the sand, creating an incongruous profile above half a million cornstalks.

Both maze owners have also extended their passion for mazes to create Maze Courtyards, which boast yet more mazes – including 'Six Minute' mazes (see pp. 222–47) – alongside the maize maze. Both have innovated by introducing extra goals, offering refreshments and even public conveniences along the way – very convenient in mazes of this scale!

DAVIS MEGAMAZE
1999

opposite In 1999 the Pirate theme ran through the entire Davis Megamaze, from the plan of a skull and two sabres, to the Victory Bridge made to look like the deck of a ship, complete with masts and shot-through sails.

right In 2000, the same field at Davis Megamaze portrayed an alien Flying Saucer. The theme stimulated a great deal of recycling and welding of satellite dishes and other bizarre hardware to create a totally immersive experience for visitors.

2000

133

VERTICAL MAZES

In 2001, the Dinosaur theme included a giant Tyrannosaurus Rex plan, while the Double-Decker bridge followed the outline shape of a Stegosaurus. In 2002, opposite, 'Spies and Espionage' was the theme. When getting lost is the challenge, the art of orienteering is intended to provide the answer. This giant compass could only partly guide visitors through their spy network that included crossing the central bridge three times.

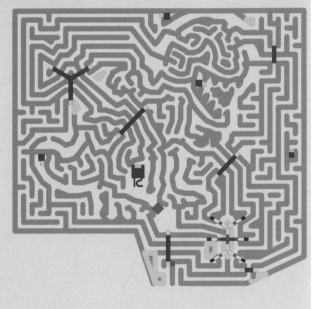

2001

2002

TULLEYS FARM
1998

The series of designs in the same field at Tulleys Farm demonstrate the continuing evolution of the maize maze as an artform. We have never hesitated to rotate the image around within the field, so some of the views are from different directions, but always of the same field. In the two years on

1999

this spread, we created a fearsome dragon, and a marvellous pirate ship; below a crew of young pirates race along the Victory Bridge, leaving some of their friends behind on a sandy desert island…in the middle of an English farmer's field.

2001

2000

2002

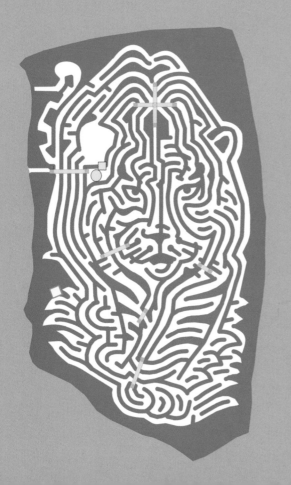

Numerous images of castles on clouds began to appear in cornfields across England and America during 2000 (opposite, left), all based around an amusing story about Merlin inventing castles that were lighter than air and could be made to fly. The barrelling on the castle towers was particularly satisfying. Tulleys Farm pioneered the world's first Y-shaped bridge in a corn maze; further innovations at Tulleys Farm were the world's first X-shaped bridge in a corn maze, and a half-way goal as well as a final goal. All these design considerations had to be worked in, without detracting from the overall image of a cowboy with lasso on his rearing horse (opposite, right), in 2001. The prowling tiger on this page, meanwhile, from 2002, became one of our most powerful maze designs, using the same distinctively shaped field, but viewed from yet another direction.

ADRIAN FISHER'S GLOBAL MAIZE MAZE ADVENTURES

The following maize mazes give an idea of the range, diversity and sheer creativity that goes into this seasonal artform. Although they take up acres in real life, they work just as well as finger mazes for you to try at home!

The Alice-in-Wonderland story is an ideal narrative for a maze, and this design works well both as a challenging maze puzzle and as an immediately recognizable image (which also worked well on T-shirts and mugs). The images of Alice, the White Rabbit, Cheshire Cat, Flamingo, Teapot, Ace of Clubs and Ace of Hearts can all be clearly seen within the design. This was the second time we had used the Alice story for a maze (see pp. 76–9), though the approach seen here is radically different to the one taken at Bournemouth, where a central mound dominates, since cornfields have to be flat.

ALICE IN WONDERLAND
ENCHANTED OAK FARM, HERTS, ENGLAND

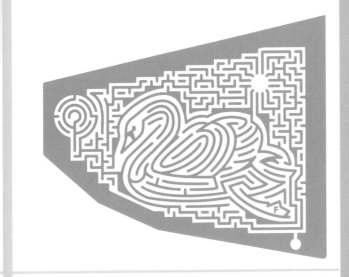

TREVISKER FARM MAZE
CORNWALL, ENGLAND

Our 2004 international theme was a space adventure, based around a space dog Fyndo who got separated from his family; visitors had to solve a quiz trail that would help Fyndo get reunited with his feckless family somewhere in outer space. Dozens of space-related maze designs were created, ranging from space stations to this design of the Solar System, which also looked like the crop circles of south west England.

FISHWICK SWAN MAZE
BERWICK, SCOTLAND

Each year, farmers choose whether to follow the international theme or select a local theme relevant to their location. This maze, near to Berwick-upon-Tweed, lies close to the border between England and Scotland, and so in 2003 used the maze to celebrate 400 years since the Union of the Crowns of England and Scotland. In 2004, Berwick's famous swans became the subject of the Fishwick maze design. In 2005 it celebrated 200 years since the Battle of Trafalgar. On average the Fishwick mazes take around two hours to solve.

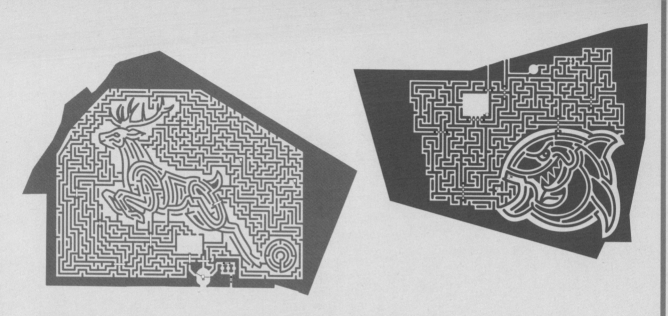

STEWARTS GARDEN LANDS MAZES
CHRISTCHURCH, ENGLAND

Martin Stewart and his team at Stewarts Garden Lands set two Guinness Records for the world's largest maze in two successive years in the same field.

In 2002, a New Forest Deer leapt into the record books covering 16 acres with 5 kilometres (8 miles) of paths, only to be surpassed the following year by a gigantic Lobster covering 19 acres. These two mazes were so large that each year the challenge was divided into three interweaving 3D networks of paths, with families carrying Silver, Gold and Platinum flags as they tackled each part of the puzzle. Their 2004 design was this playful Shark Maze.

THE WINDMILL MAZE
MILLETS FARM CENTRE
OXFORDSHIRE, ENGLAND

Britain's first cornfield maize maze in 1996 shot straight into the Guinness Book of World Records by setting a new maze world record. The design of this windmill is 'anatomically correct' with four asymmetrical sails, distinctive rotating roof, and curling clouds worthy of Van Gogh!

TROPICAL FISH MAZE
BULL RUN FARM,
ILLINOIS, USA

This tropical fish maze was one of many enchanting designs in 2003 created on an underwater theme. A fanciful story set families the challenge of finding out why the world's coral reefs seemed to be disappearing; it turned out that a gigantic undersea monster was hungry, having run out of his favourite diet of jelly beans, so he had been munching his way through brightly coloured coral reefs instead. Having solved this mystery, children (and any undersea monsters) were rewarded with jelly beans at the goal. Like many of these mazes, it includes the Adrian Fisher Mazes distinctive circular logo in the background of the image, like a 'watermark'.

143

TEXEL MAZE
TEXEL ISLAND, THE NETHERLANDS

Texel Island is in the North Sea and is the largest of the offshore islands of the Netherlands. It is a wonderful holiday island, with many miles of sand dunes and cycle paths. Paul van Heerwaarden uses the maize maze design each year to highlight aspects of the island, including its famous seals, its tall lighthouse, and the distinctive architecture of its principal town at the centre of the island. The benign climate and soil of Texel Island proves ideal for growing maize corn – indeed, it grows so fast that it rapidly exceeds head-height, and visitors find it difficult to see the rows of maze pathways, even from the bridges. A tower of greater height provides the best vantage point across the entire maze.

TRACTOR MAZE
BRIMSTAGE HALL
LEVERHULME
CHESHIRE, ENGLAND

One of the strong appeals of a maize maze is that it provides an authentic encounter with the living and working countryside, where visitors walk on the actual soil of the field, rather than on specially prepared gravel footpaths. The economic realities of farming that have drawn them into diversification in the first place are evident in this maze pattern: sponsorship revenue involved the sponsoring company's tractor and logo in the design.

JOUSTER MAZE
LA HOUGUE FARM
ISLAND OF JERSEY

The Island of Jersey, in the English Channel, off the coast of France, has two impressive mazes – this and the Jersey Water Maze (see pp. 176–8). Though the population is relatively small, at La Hougue Farm, Carlton and Kris LeFeuvre have created a popular

attraction around their award-winning maize maze by adding a tremendous range of children's activities which encourage local children to return several times each summer.

The Ferme de Gally is the 'home farm' of the Palace of Versailles, where the gardens were designed by Le Nôtre. In 2000 the maize maze marked the two-hundredth anniversary of his death by reworking one of Le Nôtre's maze designs. The following year, 2001, a Wild West theme was interpreted in the image of a cowboy riding a bucking bronco, complete with lassoo.

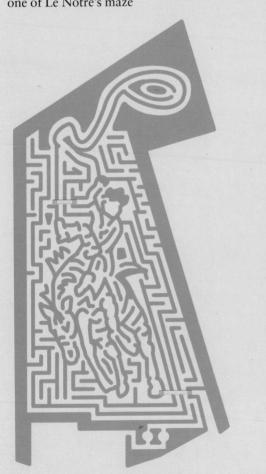

COWBOY AND 'LE NÔTRE' MAZES
FERME DE GALLY, VERSAILLES, FRANCE

SHIELD MAZE
SMEATON FARM
CORNWALL, ENGLAND

Since Smeaton Farm is rented from the Duchy of Cornwall (whose head is the Prince of Wales), it was an intriguing challenge to design a maze in the form of the shield with fifteen circles that is the heraldic emblem of Cornwall. The maze is particularly teasing since the circles all look the same.

SPACEMAN MAZE
POSTERN HOUSE FARM
STAFFS., ENGLAND

Another of our space maze designs, to complement rocket, planet and alien mazes elsewhere, was this astronaut in a space suit performing a space walk. Many miles below him, the curvature of the earth can be seen. The goal in this puzzle is his left boot.

DINOSAUR MAZE
REDHOUSE FARM, MANCHESTER, ENGLAND

Jonny Hewitt is one of England's leading exponents of farm diversification, with activities ranging from parties and Halloween events to a gigantic walk-through inflatable called The Beast. Partly in deference to this, his chosen image in 2005 was a Tyrannosaurus Rex. The design uses a four-way crossover bridge to add an extra puzzle challenge, since there are three high-level routes to choose from when you reach the centre of this bridge, as well as similar choices offered below at ground level.

BELVEDERE PLANTATION MAZES
FREDERICKSBURG, VIRGINIA, USA

Donnie Fulks's own character plays a great part in each year's corn maze at Belvedere Plantation. For the first maze, he wanted to try something new: to have a design where visitors started in the middle. The result was a convincing perspective image, with the distant castle towers seeming to disappear into the background. Each year the design process revealed more of Donnie's character. Another year when creating a Wild West design we reflected the time when Donnie had got caught in a cattle stampede – the result was an image of a herd of stampeding cattle across eight acres of cornfield.

The maze designs at Belvedere Plantation are among the most inventive anywhere. Clockwise, from right: 'Great Pumpkin Maze (2005); 'Stampede' (2001); 'Castle' (2000); 'Bungle in the Jungle' (2002).

HAMPSHIRE MEGAMAZE
PORTSMOUTH, HAMPSHIRE, ENGLAND

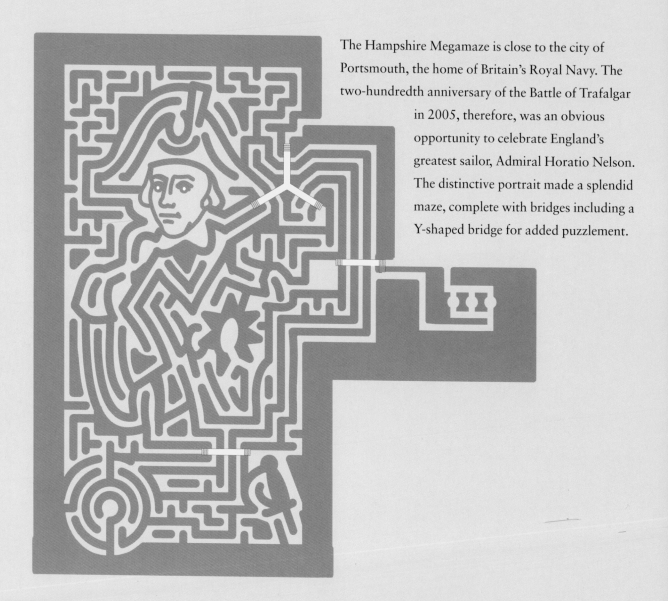

The Hampshire Megamaze is close to the city of Portsmouth, the home of Britain's Royal Navy. The two-hundredth anniversary of the Battle of Trafalgar in 2005, therefore, was an obvious opportunity to celebrate England's greatest sailor, Admiral Horatio Nelson. The distinctive portrait made a splendid maze, complete with bridges including a Y-shaped bridge for added puzzlement.

FIELD OF DREAMS
PENNSYLVANIA USA

Maize cornfields are one of the enduring features of the American landscape, immortalized (and inseparably connected with) the game of baseball by the movie *Field of Dreams*. This maize maze was created on the actual farm where the film was made, and portrays 'Shoeless' Joe Jackson, one of the all-time heroes of baseball. The commercial opportunity was not lost of including the name of a sponsor at the foot of the design.

FRANKLIN PARK
COLUMBUS OHIO

This is one of the smallest maize mazes ever created, covering just one acre, and also a rare example of a maize maze created within a city. It was planted on an open space adjacent to the Franklin Park Conservatory, and was intended to provide an educational experience for school parties, complete with a series of panels forming a Quiz Trail.

COWBOY AND GALLEON MAZES
HIDCOTE, GLOUCESTERSHIRE, ENGLAND

Each year John Wrighton has a maize maze on his farm, adjacent to the famous National Trust gardens of Hidcote Manor. Although his field – and therefore his maze design – is the same shape and size each year, close inspection of these two designs reveals that the Galleon Maze (2005) has more bridges than the Cowboy Maze (2001), evidence that John adds bridges each year to improve his maze. The Cowboy Maze had a Y-shaped bridge, while the Galleon had an X-shaped bridge, both offering an enjoyable choice of routes when high above the cornfield.

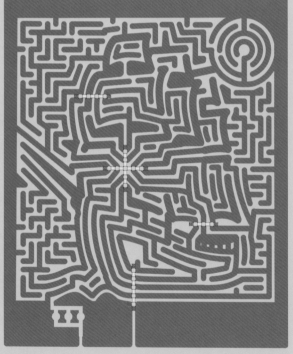

STAR AND SINGER MAZES
HEATHERTON COUNTRY PARK, SOUTH WALES

Whether an abstract Star pattern, or an immediately recognizable tribute to Elvis, the maze as an artform offers endless possibilities. Heatherton Country Park is in the beautiful unspoilt countryside of Pembrokeshire, far from any major city or centre of population, and therefore it aims to attract holidaymakers to visit its maze.

CHERRY CREST FARM
PARADISE, PENNSYLVANIA, USA

Cherry Crest Farm had its first maize maze in 1996, and is the longest-established location to host a maize maze every year since. Adrian Fisher Mazes designed the mazes for the first four years, including the distinctive designs of Locomotive (1996, opposite), Amish Horse-Drawn Buggy (1997), Noah's Ark (1998, opposite) and Liberty Bell (1999). The maze field lies adjacent to the track of the historic Strasburg Railroad, so visitors can arrive by steam train. Jack Coleman often covers the adjacent field with colourful floral planting, such as a giant rainbow to complement the Noah's Ark maze.

CHUCKWAGON MAZE
REASEHEATH, CHESHIRE, ENGLAND

The classic American chuckwagon (left) was an obvious choice during 2001's Wild West theme, and this bold image really leaps out of the design. The American chuckwagon was the nineteenth-century equivalent of the automobile – four wheels and the freedom to go wherever you chose! For many others, the chuckwagon was the unforgiving means of travelling west for hundreds of miles across the Midwest, as pioneering settlers sought land of their own to farm.

LATTIN FARMS MAZE
FALLON, NEVADA, USA

Rick Lattin and his family have been creating a maize maze each year since 1998. For the first few years, for maximum publicity value each maze was in the distinctive shape of the state of Nevada. However, the design in 2005 was a typical American farming scene (opposite), showing a barn with its doors, hayloft and characteristic truncated roof, grain silo, tree, lines of planted crops and the warmth of the sun in the sky. The Y-shaped bridge adds to the puzzlement, while the straight Victory Bridge provides a quick exit after reaching the goal.

NORTH GEORGIA MAIZE
MAZE CLEVELAND, USA

Maize maze designs are typically two-dimensional patterns or literal images, but occasionally they portray perspective images (see also the creations at Belvedere Plantation, pp. 150–53). Seen from the sky from most angles the image may seem virtually unintelligible, but once it is seen from the intended direction the design suddenly leaps into focus and the perspective effect is spectacular. John Callaham chose an orienteering compass for his maze design in 2005, as a motif symbolizing exploration and personal navigation in the outdoors and wilderness.

MIRROR MAZES + OTHER VERTICAL MAZES

Experimenting with the barrier material can produce very different mazes. Mirror and even water and inflatable plastic have all been used to create fresh challenges and even more demanding puzzles.

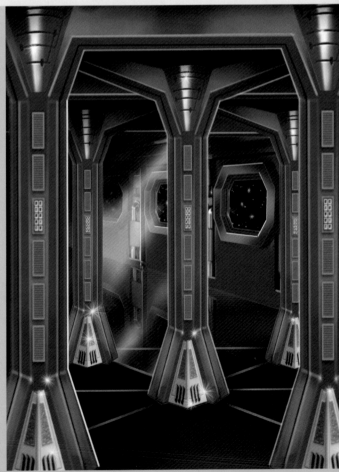

While the essential experiences of a hedge maze and maize maze are in many respects fairly similar, mirror mazes offer something genuinely different – not least because a mirror maze appears up to six times larger than it actually is. The earliest mirror maze appeared in Constantinople in 1889; the world's oldest surviving example, the Petrin Mirror Maze in Prague in the Czech Republic, dates back to 1891, and another fine example, from 1896, can be found in the Glacier Gardens, Lucerne, Switzerland. More than a dozen mirror mazes were built in America at amusement parks and fairgrounds during the first half of the twentieth century.

For several decades there was little interest in the form, but in 1991 the mirror maze underwent a metamorphosis and began a renaissance, beginning with the maze at Wookey Hole Caves in England, and subsequently spreading worldwide. These modern mirror mazes use wider mirrors, multiple thematic episodes and imaginative storylines, combined with compelling tableaux, illusions, soundtracks and lighting effects, to achieve unprecedented experiences. The number of mirror mazes worldwide has increased four-fold since 1991.

But mirror mazes are not the only thing to be excited about. Water is always fascinating, so a maze consisting entirely of walls of water, as at the Jersey Water Maze, is pure heaven! And new inflatable mazes can now take the maze experience to every place imaginable.

opposite, left Enchanted Dragon Mirror Maze, Skyline Caverns, Virginia, USA
opposite, right Space Adventure Mirror Maze, IMAX Theatre, Hyderabad, India
above, left Drummer Boy, Edinburgh Dungeon Mirror Maze
above, right Enchanted Garden Mirror Maze, Ibn Battuta Mall, Dubai, UAE

MAGICAL MIRROR MAZE
WOOKEY HOLE CAVES, SOMERSET, ENGLAND

In early 1991, Peter Haylings was looking for a new attraction for Wookey Hole Caves that would complement and enhance his existing Victorian 'Fairground by Night' exhibition and Edwardian 'Penny Pier Arcade' attractions. We met and agreed that a mirror maze based on the old portable mirror mazes that accompanied travelling fairgrounds would be an inspired solution. Our research included visits to the Glacier Gardens mirror maze in Lucerne, and a remarkable machine of rotating mirrors, formerly in the Musée Grevin in Paris. A completely new concept was developed, with wider mirrors than ever previously attempted, so wide apart that visitors could not touch mirrors on both sides simultaneously; the spectacular effect on visitors was intended to create, and achieved, total disorientation! The chosen soundtrack captured the carefree atmosphere of an Edwardian seaside pier with exuberant children, swooping seagulls and a distant brass band.

DRAGON MAZE

PEAUGRES SAFARI PARK, NR LYONS, FRANCE

Viscount Paul de la Panouse was keen to enhance his collection of live pythons, scorpions and bats housed beneath his château at Peaugres Safari Park in the Ardeches Mountains (as well as adding to his collection of mazes at the châteaux of Thoiry, pp. 68–71, and Colombier, p. 94). This called for a grand design uniting the creative talents of patron, architect and maze designer, which opened in 1994.

We created a new terrace in front of the château complete with an 'infinity pool', with the lip of the pool peeling away as the crest of a waterfall. The waterfall cascades over a rugged rock façade into a deep ravine. Visitors approach from below by crossing a footbridge across the ravine, and passing dry through the waterfall which separates in two without getting them wet. Beneath the terrace, they enter an extended basement containing a pool of live crocodiles; the only way forward is across a glass-sided bridge over the crocodile pool.

Finally visitors enter the mirror maze, decorated in the style of an Egyptian Temple after the Great Labyrinth of Ancient Egypt. Hieroglyphs and vibrant Egyptian colours adorn the pillars. Tanks of aquarium fish appear all around. At one point, a crash of breaking glass is following by the sudden apparition of the front half of a crocodile on the maze floor, while his hind legs still seem to be within the crocodile pool!

KING ARTHUR'S MIRROR MAZE
LONGLEAT, ENGLAND

If stately homes and castles did not have lead roofs, which are so expensive to maintain, I am convinced there would be twice as many mazes. Accordingly, aware that Alexander Lord Bath has five acres of lead roofs, I had always approached the Longleat estate with trepidation. How could the frivolity of a maze compete with the financial burden of such extensive maintenance? Fortunately Alexander Bath is a great maze enthusiast – before he succeeded his father as Lord Bath, he had commissioned Greg Bright in 1974 to create a hedge maze at Longleat of unprecedented size and complexity (see pp. 58–61). King Arthur's Mirror Maze, which opened in 1998, was the fifth maze on the estate at Longleat.

Visitors are invited to imagine they are knights who have set off to perform a Quest. On their journey through the dark forest, they encounter Excalibur, the sword in the stone, which mysteriously appears, rises, rotates, descends and disappears from sight. The half-hidden faces of Green Men stare out at them from the branches of trees. Wild sounds, and the occasional tolling of a bell, ring through the forest. Fog swirls around visitors as they penetrate deeper into the unknown. Lightning and thunder echo around them. They reach a ruined chapel. The Round Table, symbol of their noble order, can be seen suspended between gothic arches. The thunderstorm continues to rage, seen through a stained glass window. Finally within the chapel, they may find the Holy Grail, but only if they are pure in heart (or know how to make it appear!). This maze was a breakthrough in mirror maze design, in part because the layout of the mirrors departs from the traditional arrangement of equilateral triangles, to produce a remarkable effect which eliminates long straight arcades of arches.

Green Men – ancient woodland spirits – haunt the impressively three-dimensional trees, while the final goal of the Quest – a ruined Gothic chapel, above – creates a wonderful sense of place. Mirror mazes offer a perfect immersive environment, which is taken to a new extreme in this maze. At the very end, the visitor conjures the Holy Grail.

LONDON DUNGEON MIRROR MAZE
ENGLAND

The London Dungeon is one of five Dungeons across Europe to have a mirror maze, the others being in Hamburg, Amsterdam, Edinburgh and York. Each is based on a local story – in Edinburgh the Drummer Boy, at London the lost spirit of Spitalfields who desperately scratched lettering with her fingernails.

AMAZING CHICAGO NAVY PIER, CHICAGO, USA

'Amazing Chicago' is a vivacious celebration of the city of Chicago and its love affair with skyscrapers. It contains two distinct mirror maze experiences to portray different levels of the Chicago landscape. Dark underground subway tunnels seem to continue endlessly beneath the city (seen below).

Then, at ground level, visitors experience an Alice in Wonderland-like transformation as they walk like giants between tall models of Chicago's stunning architectural landmarks, whose city blocks seem to stretch to infinity.

ENCHANTED GARDEN MAZE IBN BATTUTA MALL, DUBAI

Ibn Battuta was an Arab explorer and trader centuries ago, who travelled the world to many countries and cultures. This mirror maze was created to celebrate this hero as part of the launch of the Ibn Battuta Mall in Dubai, the largest

shopping mall in the world. The mirror maze contained three thematic episodes – a Conservatory, a Royal Palace and a Forest of Palm Trees. Each window arch around its perimeter contained a different colourful tessellation using the Mitre Tiling System.

RIPLEYS MIRROR MAZE PATTAYA, THAILAND

This impressive mirror maze in Pattaya consists of a series of chambers, each offering a different experience. Strictly speaking the White Room is a misnomer, since white is only one of its manifestations; its walls are covered in tessellation patterns using the Mitre Tiling System, behind which a changing sequence of pastel lights creates an ethereal effect. By contrast, the Infinity Room (bottom) overcomes one of the classic challenges of Infinity Rooms that have taxed mirror-maze designers since the late nineteenth century. Visitors feel they are in infinite space in three dimensions, just like the squadrons of fish in one of M. C. Escher's memorable drawings.

JERSEY WATER MAZE
ST HELIER, JERSEY, CHANNEL ISLANDS

Opened in 1997, this water maze is now one of the key features installed within Les Jardins de la Mer, St Helier, on the island of Jersey in the English Channel Islands. This remarkable maze includes 208 fountain jets which rise and fall to create walls of water, in the form of a maze whose design is constantly changing as visitors walk through it. A dolphin sculpture by Philip Jackson, set within a 6-metre (20-foot) diameter pool, lies at the centre of the maze.

Measuring 19 metres (62 feet) across, this maze is a major design breakthrough, taking the use of walls of water further than ever before. 'Time' itself becomes an extra dimension, as the walls change their configuration from second to second. The fountains consist of 18 giant foaming pillars, each rising up to 2.5 metres (8 feet) high, and a further 190 thinner fountain jets. The fountains are computer-controlled, and linked together into groups. Using precision valve technology, originally developed for nuclear submarines, the heights and timing of the fountains can be controlled much more precisely than ever before. These elaborate arrangements, hidden in the underground control room, allow the maze to run a varied thirty-minute sequence without repeating itself.

As night falls, fibre optic lighting within the water jets illuminates the pillars of water. The maze becomes a magical spectacle to watch, even if no one is within the maze.

AN INFLATABLE MAZE
LOCATION VARIABLE

Inflatable mazes are the ultimate form of instant and transportable maze, ideal for events and festivals, and involve a completely new set of design considerations. This form of maze design ingeniously transfers its compressed air overhead, with supporting pillars deriving air pressure from above and simply resting on the ground. Since no one walks on the fabric, the material can be finer and lighter, and therefore packs down to a remarkably small volume for transportation.

With their height and colourful fabric creating a dramatic visual impact, these inflatable mazes are very popular with younger families, since parents can go in with their children, and no one has to take their shoes off. Once inside, the repetition of bright curving corridors creates instant bafflement; as an added extra, there are changeable Quiz Challenges, so that the inflatable maze has not one but perhaps half a dozen or more goals to reach.

THE MAZE AS AN ARTFORM

There are many parallels between the creation of a maze and a piece of sculpture. Both artforms are first conceived in the mind's eye, to convey or celebrate an idea, and to achieve a transforming experience. Early discussions, sketches and photomontages may lead on to maquettes, prototypes and studio models, as the concept and detailed designs go through their numerous revisions. The practical aspects of fabrication and construction require mastery of the chosen technology and materials, while composition and colour are of paramount importance. The final result should intrigue, entice, engage and move its visitors.

And as in any artistic field of endeavour, there is a limit to the resources of the artist himself to fund the creation of a substantial collection, particularly when his ideas keep running forward faster than the effort of bringing each idea to fruition. So at least part of the output must be used to generate revenue, through fees, outright sale, rental, patronage or sponsorship.

Perhaps paradoxically then, in this modern age, the creative process still relies on that centuries-old personal relationship of Artist and Patron, of portrait painter and sitter, just as much as in the Renaissance. The artist helps the 'sitter' relax and express himself – and then like lightning he pounces and captures that spirit on canvas! However, the patron's input is also an important part of the creative process, again just as in portraiture, where a certain aspect of somebody's character will be emphasized. For the maze designer, sparring to stretch and achieve a creative result with each successive owner is the overriding goal at that moment in time. Of course, the modern-day patron differs from his Renaissance counterpart in crucial ways, and is today more likely to be the Director of a zoo or museum, or the President of a theme park (though private commissions remain particularly vital to the development of the artist's career). But the fundamental creative relationship remains unchanged.

As with any artist, the work of a maze designer tends to evolve over their career, as one idea is developed and leads on to another. The same landscape at the beginning and end of a working life can engender radically different responses in the same artist. Indeed, originality and innovation are essential to the maze-making process. And as with all artists, the maze maker sees no artistic purpose in mass production of any one achievement, but prefers to work with each location to create a custom-designed installation. In a repetitive world, the spirit soars when confronted with a unique example of a maze with appropriate symbolism, specially designed for its setting. When prospective patrons look through my previous designs, much of what they see they can't have – but equally, whatever is uniquely designed for them will never be repeated.

All maze designers revel in the challenges offered by the most varied of requirements. Donnie Fulks wants his corn maze each year to start in the middle. At Three Lands Point, Jean Jannsen and I wanted to create maze gates that could open and close from moment to moment, yet without jamming children's fingers in the hinges (so we used pillars of foaming water). To cope with heavy numbers of visitors to the Archbishop's Maze at Greys Court, Randoll Coate and I reversed the role of grass within the turf maze, so that the grass became the barrier and the path became three rows of brick. The aesthetic effect was very pleasing, and so a new form of maze was born. The sixteenth-century waterfall you can walk behind at the Villa d'Este near Rome finds its maze counterpart at Legoland Windsor. Creating a maze in a cornfield allows a different design and theme each year, thus stimulating creativity season after season.

Like any other three-dimensional artform, the maze experience is intended to intrigue, entice, engage and have an effect on its visitors, leaving them transformed by the encounter. Several of my own creations are large enough to be seen on Google Earth. On this largest artistic scale, the maze has the unique ability to absorb into itself complete groups of visitors, and then subject them to an unfolding, unstructured and unique experience where they are free to make choices and decisions in their journey of exploration and discovery.

In 1986 Randoll Coate wrote 'Seven Golden Rules for Making a Maze' which combined his characteristic enthusiasm, optimism and wit. His seventh rule stated: 'Do not allow the cost of the maze to cloud your enjoyment of a creation which will bring pleasure to young and old for generations to come. You will have given our world of harsh reality and mindless speed a timeless oasis, a leisurely paradise, the substance of a dream.'

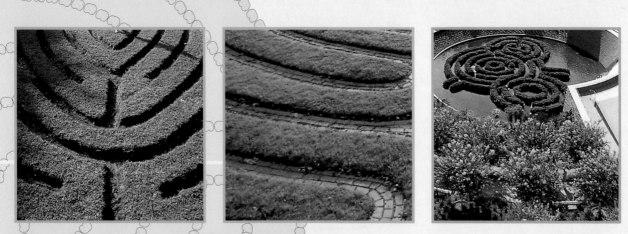

HORIZONTAL MAZES

Two-dimensional mazes are designed to be walked upon, to provide a space for informal play, and to breathe life into the landscape. Whatever the setting, the choice of materials is crucial to the character of the maze. The horizontal format is ideal for contemplative labyrinths, whether created as a spiritual focus for a church or community, a memorial for a loved one, or as a place of healing or meditation. However, the fact that the maze is two-dimensional does not mean any compromise to creativity.

TURF MAZES **+**
PATH-IN-GRASS MAZES

One of the oldest forms of maze design, these mazes and labyrinths use natural materials to create a simple and meaningful puzzle or path.

This section looks at two closely related maze forms, one the inverse of the other. Of the two, turf labyrinths are by far the older version, dating back many centuries. In them, the visitor walks on the grass, and typically they are unicursal. For all their simplicity they create a wonderful effect and make a great contribution to the landscape.

Turf labyrinths are typically found on village greens, on wide grassy roadside verges and in open countryside, as an informal community activity, belonging outside private formal gardens. The labyrinth, with its clear symbolism as a Path of Life, the thread of time from birth to death, provided a potent metaphor, a compelling visual image, a competitive challenge and an outlet for physical energy. Historically, turf labyrinths developed across northern Europe; in England eight ancient turf labyrinths survive from perhaps as many

above Chester Path-in-Grass Maze, England
opposite Wing turf labyrinth, Rutland, England

as one hundred suggested by distinctive and characteristic place names. Three examples have also survived in Germany, with another recently restored there.

Yet the problem with turf mazes is that everyone is required to walk on the grass, and even moderate numbers of visitors rapidly wear out the central strip. An alternative is to reverse the roles of the grass and the strip in between, so that the grass strip becomes the barrier, as had happened at St Catherine's Hill, Winchester, and Saffron Walden. I developed this idea and used it to create the world's first paved 'path-in-grass' maze, at Greys Court (see pp. 188–93). This new form proved very successful, and I went on to use it in a number of the projects shown here.

SAFFRON WALDEN MAZE
SAFFRON WALDEN, ENGLAND

This ancient turf labyrinth, from 1699, in the form of a large circle with four 'bastions', is unusual in having a narrow single row of embedded bricks, which has left the adjacent grass untrodden and in good condition. The largest surviving turf labyrinth in the world, it measures approximately 40 metres (132 feet) across. The central mound originally had an ash tree, but this was burned down on Guy Fawkes Night, 1823. The earliest drawing of the maze dates to 1768.

TULLEYS FARM TURF MAZE
WEST SUSSEX, ENGLAND

This turf labyrinth was created as part of the first maize maze at Tulleys Farm in 1998. Each year, Stuart Beare and his team maintain it by mowing and trench clearing, to keep its pristine appearance. With 30,000 or more visitors each summer, it is interesting to see how the grass paths stand up to the sheer weight of numbers. Over time, we have come to terms with the same issues faced by the medieval creators, specifically how to make the grass as resistant as possible.

THE ARCHBISHOP'S MAZE
GREYS COURT, OXFORDSHIRE, ENGLAND

Lady Brunner commissioned The Archbishop's Maze in 1980, having been inspired by the words of Dr Robert Runcie, who, during his enthronement sermon when becoming Archbishop of Canterbury, described a dream of a maze: 'There were some people very close to the centre, but they could not find a way through. Just outside the maze others were standing. They were further away from the heart of the maze, but they would be there sooner than the party that fretted and fumed inside.'

Randoll Coate and I created this maze abounding in Christian symbolism, with its cruciform shape, the image of the Crown of Thorns, the Seven Days of Creation, Nine Hours of Agony and Twelve Apostles. At the centre, a simple Roman cross of Bath stone is laid within an elaborate Byzantine cross of blue Westmorland stone. These proclaim the reconciliation between East and West, Catholic and

Protestant, Roman and Orthodox – a vital aspect of Dr Runcie's life work. In one sense, the maze is a puzzle, and there are various junctions with choices to be made. However, by crossing straight over each diamond-shaped thorn, one walks the entire quarter mile path of the maze. This route represents the Christian Path of Life. Attractive as turf mazes are, they cannot cope with heavy numbers of visitors, so for the maze at this National Trust property we reversed the role of grass within the maze, so that the path was three rows of brick and grass became the barrier. Just before the centre is an inscription: 'This maze was dedicated by Robert Runcie, Archbishop of Canterbury, 24 October 1981.' At the centre an armillary sundial is supported by a stone pillar, inscribed with lines from Saint Augustine, Julian of Norwich, Siegfried Sassoon and Robert Gittings.

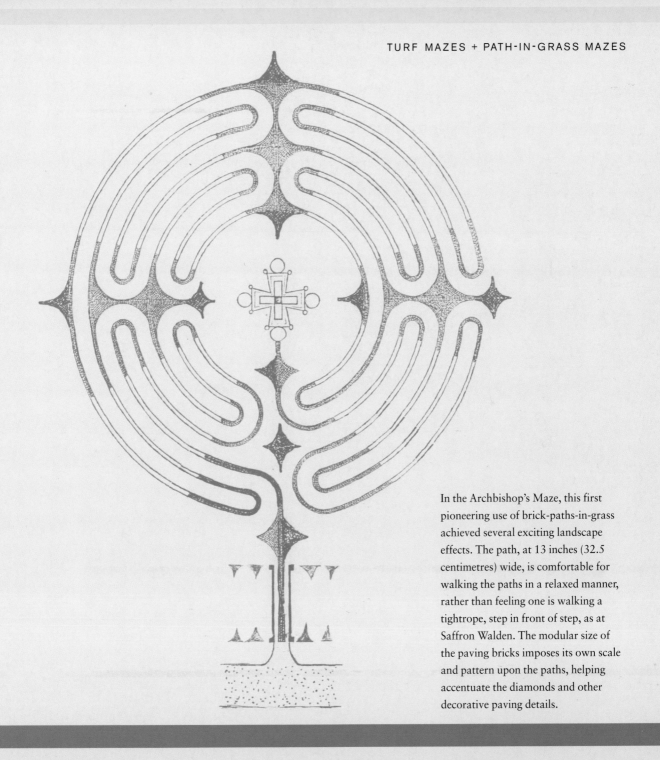

In the Archbishop's Maze, this first pioneering use of brick-paths-in-grass achieved several exciting landscape effects. The path, at 13 inches (32.5 centimetres) wide, is comfortable for walking the paths in a relaxed manner, rather than feeling one is walking a tightrope, step in front of step, as at Saffron Walden. The modular size of the paving bricks imposes its own scale and pattern upon the paths, helping accentuate the diamonds and other decorative paving details.

There is a wonderful textural contrast
between the man-made hard paving
and the natural living turf. This
contrast goes through subtle changes
as the lawn grows day by day and its
height gradually rises, until it is time
to be mown again; seen at a low angle
when walking the maze, as in this
photograph, this maze clearly still has
a vertical dimension, as the curving
paths are gradually obscured by the
higher grass strips. The brick path is
also set into the oak bridge at the
beginning, seen here on the left.

JULIAN'S BOWER
ALKBOROUGH, LINCOLNSHIRE, ENGLAND

Some turf mazes can be very ancient. This example in Lincolnshire, 13.4 metres (44 feet) across, is thought to date to around the year 1200, when it was cut by monks from the local Benedictine monastery. Such mazes, which are often unicursal, originally also had a religious meaning, though as late as the nineteenth century they were also still being used for 'May-eve' games. Over time the maze has come to define the village, and the parish church has a replica of the maze in the floor of the south porch and in the stained glass of the chancel window. A clue to the mastermind behind these last two mazes lies in Alkborough cemetery, where the same maze design appears yet again on the tombstone of Mr J. Goulton-Constable.

METAMORPHOSIS TURF MAZE
NORTON MUSEUM OF ART, FLORIDA, USA

In 1997 the Norton Museum of Art hosted a one-man show of my work as a maze designer. As part of the exhibition, I created this turf maze in the shape of an egg, which was accompanied by a 100-metre (300-foot) long grass mound coiling round the egg in the form of a Serpent. The whole thus symbolizes the cycle of life, from Egg to Serpent, and Serpent to Egg. My maze exhibition occupied two indoor galleries including floor colour mazes, together with a Rope Maze in an outer courtyard, and in the East Garden a permanent brick pavement maze depicting Theseus slaying the Minotaur, which is illustrated on p. 215.

VERONICA'S MAZE
PARHAM PARK, PULBOROUGH, SUSSEX, ENGLAND

This maze with its quarter mile of brick paths was built on the lawn where the owner Veronica Tritton used to play and ride her bicycle as a girl. It achieves the delightful effect of creating close-up decorative detail in the foreground, without causing any kind of vertical obstruction to the broader landscape view beyond. It can be enjoyed in wet weather since the paths remain firm and do not become slippery or turn to mud.

Nowhere in the design is there a straight line, since the plan was inspired by a sixteenth-century embroidery over the Great Bed within the house. This was the first 'one-way' puzzle maze created in the landscape with the rule that once you have started walking, you must keep going forwards and never turn back on yourself. Like a railway track, there are several diamond crossovers where you cannot turn left or right; these allow the design to function as a three-dimensional puzzle, since these diamonds behave like bridges and underpasses. The overall maze measures 30 x 18 metres (96 x 60 feet).

THE MILLENNIUM MAZE HIGGINSON PARK, MARLOW, ENGLAND

Opened in 2000, this maze lies on the banks of the River Thames, and celebrates the river in the history of Marlow. The maze paths consist of clay paving bricks laid between grass, and portray eleven fish curling and twisting, forming an intriguing maze where visitors must always walk forwards. Four areas of mosaic portray aspects of the town's history: the Vikings, the military academy, and the angling and rowing traditions.

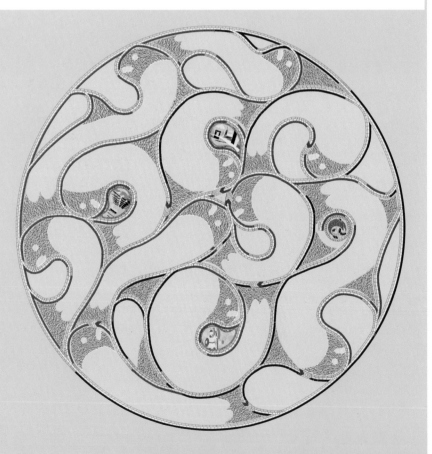

ROLAWN TURF MAZE
GATESHEAD NATIONAL GARDEN FESTIVAL, ENGLAND

Five Garden Festivals were held in Britain between 1984 (Liverpool – see p. 216) and 1992. The Gateshead Festival was held in 1988. The Rolawn Turf Maze was an interesting way to demonstrate the sculptural qualities of the sponsor's turf product as a visual artform, and it was intended to be looked down on rather than walked upon. I created a new turf maze geometry based on five-fold symmetry, with five rings of grass paths separated by gravel strips, and five bastions each containing a stone ball. This eye-catching exercise of distinct design elements was awarded a Silver Medal.

BATH FESTIVAL MAZE
BEAZER GARDENS, BATH, ENGLAND

'The Maze' was chosen as the theme for the 1984 Bath Festival, as expressed in music, opera, painting, sculpture, literature and film. As part of the Festival, it was decided to build a full-size permanent maze in the heart of the City of Bath, in the Beazer Gardens beside the River Avon, immediately below the Pulteney Bridge. Set in grass, the Bath stone paths, which measure 45 cm (15 inches) wide, describe an elegant ellipse, recalling the Georgian fanlights above the doors of the city, the Brunel railway arches and the shape of the nearby Pulteney weir. The overall dimensions are 29.5 x 22 metres (97 x 73 feet). Paradoxically the path to the goal is always shortened by taking turnings away from the centre.

The maze can also be solved by going straight over each junction, when every path in the maze is walked once and once only. At the centre is an Italian marble mosaic, 4.5 metres (15 feet) in diameter, made up of over 72,000 mosaic pieces in fifteen colours. It contains an enlarged representation of the famous Gorgon's Head of Bath, surrounded by six apses celebrating the Four Seasons, the Four Elements, and Bath's Celtic and Roman past. Its central circle ringed by six semi-circular apses echoes the central area in the labyrinth at Chartres Cathedral. Each of these seven images are 'Gaze-Mazes' in their own right – mazes solved by looking rather than walking. The maze path around the Gorgon's Head is depicted in gold Venetian glass, alluding to Aridane's golden thread. Persephone represents Bath, the City of Flowers, while Orpheus and his lyre emphasize the music of the annual Bath Festival; Blalud's herd of swine in the magic mire represent Earth; and Pegasus represents Air; the Minotaur maze stands for Fire; and the Dolphins maze, for Water.

PAVING MAZES + OTHER HORIZONTAL MAZES

Horizontal mazes can be created from many materials aside from turf. Colourful mosaic, earthy brick or hard-wearing tiles, each gives a different effect.

In the last section we saw how the ancient turf maze developed into the 'path-in-grass' maze. Just as effectively, tiles, brick and stone paving by themselves can make wonderful, challenging mazes. Paving mazes create areas of activity, acting as a special focus for play and social interaction. Many people can play on a paving maze at the same time, and they require little maintenance to look splendid. Flat, paved maze patterns can also bring to life intimate courtyards and larger surrounded spaces.

One of my great inspirations has been the tiling patterns within the Alhambra Palace in Spain, where the character and purpose of the decorative tilings come alive in their context. My journey to Granada was all the more exciting because I was retracing the steps of M. C. Escher who had visited the Alhambra Palace earlier in the century, and who spent many

opposite York Gate, Adel, Leeds, Yorkshire
above, left St John's College School, Cambridge
above, right Unicorn Rampant Maze, Worksop Town Centre, Nottinghamshire

days there observing and sketching in colour on the spot. Over time I have developed a number of tiling and paving systems that enable me to create dynamic, colourful and sophisticated patterns and puzzles anywhere.

Another compelling form of horizontal labyrinth is that made from stone boulders or rocks. Such labyrinths can remain relatively intact for centuries, unlike turf mazes which can be lost in a few years. The physical task of collecting and transporting hundreds of boulders to the chosen site creates its own geographical limitation. Historically, boulder labyrinths are associated with enchanting traditions and legends.

TUDOR ROSE MAZE KENTWELL HALL
LONG MELFORD, SUFFOLK, ENGLAND

The Wars of the Roses raged in England for much of the fifteenth century, between the Lancastrians, whose emblem was the red rose, and the Yorkists, whose emblem was the white rose. Eventually the feud was resolved by the Battle of Bosworth in 1485 and Henry VII's subsequent marriage to Elizabeth of York, and the roses were combined to created the distinctive Tudor Rose, comprised of the superimposed red and white roses.

This enormous brick pavement mosaic maze – which at 21 metres (70 feet) square is the world's largest of its kind – was installed in 1985 to commemorate the 500th anniversary of the beginning of the Tudor dynasty of 1485. Filling the main courtyard of moated Kentwell Hall, it was built with twenty-seven thousand red and white paving bricks. Set into my rose maze design are fifteen diamonds of etched brick, designed by Randoll Coate and decorated with symbols representing the Tudor dynasty. The maze design simultaneously offers a five-fold unicursal labyrinth, a maze puzzle, and, at the centre, a giant chess board. The five separate progressions through the maze, from the five outer thorns to the centre, echo the internal rotational symmetry hidden within Classical and Medieval Christian unicursal labyrinths. Alternatively, the rose becomes a three-dimensional puzzle maze, by observing junctions and flyovers indicated by the brick paths.

Without Patrick and Judith Phillips' financial commitment and lifelong dedication, Kentwell Hall would have been added to the list of over 5,000 English country houses lost since 1950. It was therefore particularly encouraging that this maze received the British Tourist Authority's 'Heritage in the Making' Award in 1985.

AMAZEING FACTS

How big is it? 455 sq m (4,900 sq ft)

How long are the paths? 300 m. (1,000 ft)

When did it open? 1985

What's it made of? Brick pavement

Did you know? This maze uses 27,000 paving bricks, which required 19,000 cuts. The laying of the maze took two twin brothers five months to complete.

ORANG-UTAN MAZE
EDINBURGH ZOO
SCOTLAND

Located at the centre of the Darwin Maze (see p. 63), this 6-metre (20-foot) square paving maze is viewed from a platform. It was created using 7-sided and 5-sided 'Edinburgh Pavers', and shows an Orang Utan. The exit path, below, is paved to look like DNA.

MALL OF GEORGIA PAVING MAZE

ATLANTA, GEORGIA, USA

The main outdoor axis of the Mall of Georgia required a spirited piece of art, yet one that would not detract from the overall view or function of the path. This lively decorative paving was the result. Set symmetrically within four low circular brick walls containing trees, the pavement design itself is anything but symmetrical. Its leitmotif is a gigantic seashell, 44 feet (13.4 metres) across, which is of necessity spiralling and asymmetrical. Within its design, there are seven 'Six Minute' mazes, each with a different puzzle rule to follow. In this way, families can sit on the low walls and play with the mazes, thus adding informal and spontaneous 'street life' to the area.

THREE PAVING MAZES
SOUTH GERMANTOWN PARK, MARYLAND, USA

South Germantown has three mazes, using different forms of brick paving. The largest maze is a One-Way Maze constructed of brick paths in grass, shown above. You 'launch' by rocket (from either side of the design) into a headlong journey through space, forever going forwards. When elliptical orbits align precisely, you can switch from one orbit to another and perform 'slingshot' accelerations around the various planets you encounter. Your goal is the Sun at the centre of the Solar System.

The second maze is an Arrow Maze laid in brick paving. Each move is a hop through the air, with you choosing the distance, and the maze dictating your direction each time you land on your next chosen square. Your goal is the central square.

The third maze is based on a Native American Indian rug design that originated from the Two

Grey Hills Trading Post in New Mexico. It is one of the few historic posts on the Navajo Indian Reservation, and remains the primary source of authentic regional rugs and tapestries, made of hand-spun yarn from the fleece of naturally coloured local sheep in shades of grey, brown, black and white. Decorative paving, tapestries and rug weaving share a common 'orthogonal' geometry based on two axes set at right angles, with the distinctive regularity of the modular design unit, and the use of a reticent range of naturally occurring colours to bring out the strength of the overall design. In this paving design, the maze paths are natural shades of red, gold and brown kiln-fired paving bricks. To solve the maze, you enter on a gold path and change path colour each time you reach a blue diamond-shaped junction.

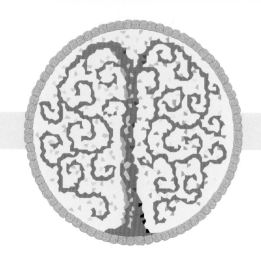

ROXBURY LABYRINTH CONNECTICUT, USA

This contemplative labyrinth on a private estate in Connecticut, was created by a couple in memory of their son. They had found solace by walking a labyrinth in California, and wanted to have one within the mature woodlands of their own garden. From the outset, the design was conceived within the context of an intimate clearing among tall trees, and the natural bedrock that rises to the surface through the estate.

The 11-metre (37-foot) diameter design uses Fisher Pavers in vibrant natural clay colours. The rugged geometry of the pavers gives the path a vigorous, changing character throughout its length. At the centre is a circular mosaic portraying the Tree of Life, made of some 3,000 pieces of Mitre Mosaic. The labyrinth design has seven concentric rings of paths, and six axes where paths double back, reflecting Hebrew geometry and numerology.

THESEUS SLAYING THE MINOTAUR
NORTON MUSEUM OF ART, WEST PALM BEACH, USA

The East Garden of the Norton Museum of Art was a splendid and yet relatively unused space outside the main courtyard, whose most notable features, two bronzes by Paul Manship of Diana and Actaeon, were installed in 1941. This paving maze was an exciting way to bring the East Garden to life. It was aligned with the central doors on the eastern façade of the museum, and one of the functions of its area of 20.1 x 13.4 metres (66 x 44 feet) was to provide a firm base for a wooden floor when the area is covered by a marquee for special events.

Classical statuary and the formal symmetry of the architecture both pointed towards the ultimate classical maze story of them all, that of Theseus slaying the Minotaur within the Cretan Labyrinth. By killing the fearsome creature, half-man and half-bull, Theseus broke the tyranny of Athens having to pay tribute to the King of Minoan Crete.

For America, the New World, having shaken off the British colonial yoke in 1776, this design in 1997 was an icon for Freedom.

The paving design contains various creative details. The perimeter Greek key pattern in a distinctive deep gold provides the rectangular border; thereafter the entire design adopts a fresh alignment at 45 degrees to the original. The outer parts of the maze are of a closer pattern, with paths two bricks wide; however the central diamond has broader paths, three bricks wide, in the manner of a magnifying glass being used to accentuate the central space. Here the fierce combat between the two central characters is so violent that horn, hand, foot and sword spill out into the wider maze beyond. Theseus raises his sword to deliver his final blow, adopting a pose found in various Roman mosaics in the centres of Roman mosaic labyrinths.

THE BEATLES MAZE
LIVERPOOL, ENGLAND

A celebration of the Beatles' outstanding musical achievement was the perfect subject for a maze at Liverpool's Garden Festival in 1984. And the obvious icon was their most fantastic musical image, the Yellow Submarine. Eighty apprentices at the Cammell Laird shipyard across the Mersey set to work creating the 18 ton, 16 metre (51 foot) long steel submarine, with spiral staircases leading up to its conning tower. Around the submarine was an aquatic pool 95 feet (29 metres) across in the shape of the Beatles' Apple, while the maze paths portrayed the ears of the world listening to the music. The Beatles Maze proved remarkably successful, and was visited by a million visitors in seven months

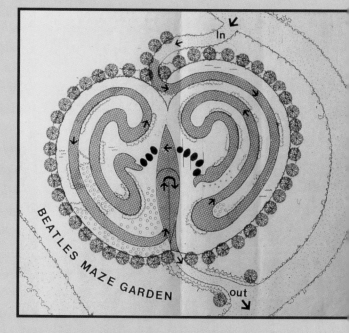

(including the Queen), and won two gold medals and a prize for the 'most innovative garden structure'.

216

FLOATING MAZE
GETTY MUSEUM, USA

This unique water maze from 1997 is horizontal in the sense that its water surface is level, and its design is intended to be looked down upon. Robert Irwin described his design as a 'floating' maze which indeed is the impression it achieves, although its azaleas are actually growing in soil within long narrow islands of cast concrete.

DOBBIES BOULDER LABYRINTH

DOBBIES MAZE
WORLD
ATHERSTONE
ENGLAND

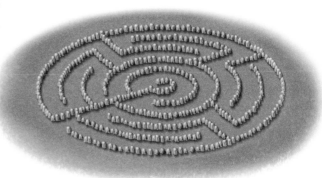

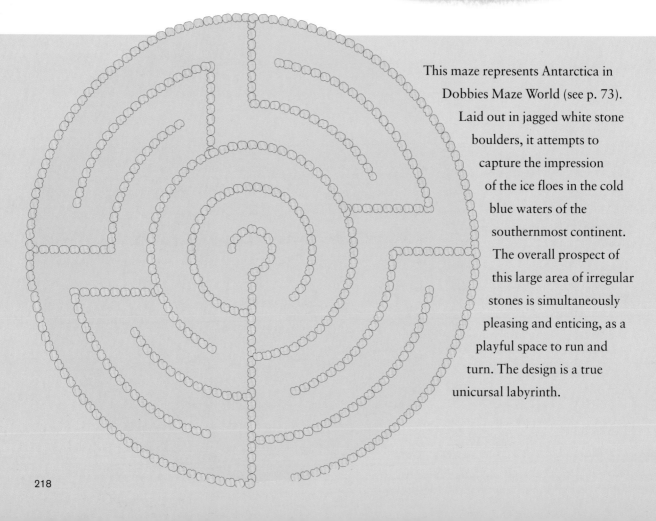

This maze represents Antarctica in Dobbies Maze World (see p. 73). Laid out in jagged white stone boulders, it attempts to capture the impression of the ice floes in the cold blue waters of the southernmost continent. The overall prospect of this large area of irregular stones is simultaneously pleasing and enticing, as a playful space to run and turn. The design is a true unicursal labyrinth.

RACHEL'S LABYRINTH GATLINBURG, USA

At 18 metres (60 feet) in diameter, this is one of the larger meditation labyrinths in the United States. Since 1991, more than 500 modern labyrinths have been created across the country, from rough stone (as here), smooth stone paving, brick paving or pressed patterned tinted concrete. Labyrinths have provided a focus for meditation and prayer in cultures around the world for thousands of years, and today there are many modern labyrinths in healthcare facilities, because the process of walking and meditation has been found to have a positive, focusing effect. This example was created by Dr Rachael Young, a founder of a wellness centre which assists cancer patients.

WHAT MAKES A GOOD MAZE?

We have already seen on pp. 180–81 how the maze is a valid artform and a distinctive element of garden and landscape design. However, while it is important that it looks good, and fits in well with its surroundings, it is equally essential that it functions well as a fascinating and challenging walk-through puzzle, as well as an all-enveloping, immersive experience.

Creating a challenging puzzle maze in whatever material, and whether on paper or in three dimensions, requires a grasp of mathematics, networks and topology. The size of the site often dictates the choice of materials and the modular scale of the paths and barriers. The overall design concept may be abstract or a symbolic image; sometimes its very geometry suggests puzzling possibilities. Gradually I develop a 'master map' of the network logic of the puzzle, rather like a national road map, leaving out the detailed twists and turns. Then I decide how the visitor experience is going to unfold, moment by moment, as visitors walk through it at ground level. The conceptual design and the puzzle logic gradually fuse together into a single entity until finally, like the crucial but ultimately redundant scaffolding being removed from a skyscraper, the elegant edifice is unveiled,

and onlookers see the end result, but not the network underpinning it.

The art of maze design also involves a consideration of timing, scale and the human attention span, so that visitors are able to solve the maze while they're still eager for more, and before they get tired and demoralized. Like optical illusions or plays performed on the radio, some of the best effects exploit the human imagination. There is a qualitative level of fulfilment that arises from mastering new ideas and learning by discovery – sometimes by trial and error, though at other times by letting visitors unconsciously choose the 'scientific method' of formulating a hypothesis and testing it by experiment.

'Six Minute' mazes, which are discussed in the next section, are challenging puzzles that lay bare the mathematical origins of mazes. They are so enjoyable and fulfilling to solve because of the high proportion of time spent assimilating the new rule, mastering it and then using it to work out a concisely expressed yet initially baffling puzzle. The same process of encounter and engagement is similar in other kinds of mazes, whether coming to terms with the size and hidden network of choices within a hedge or fence maze, or the 'impossible' paths through sheets of glass offered within a mirror maze. With time, the topology of any puzzle maze can be mastered, even when islands are introduced and the central goal is detached from the perimeter hedge, and whether the maze exists in two dimensions or three (by the addition of bridges). Yet even when the overall network structure is understood, the sheer scale of curving alleys, changes of height, one-way paths and conditional gateways can disorient and confuse the most inquisitive of explorers.

In a maze, everything is contrived, since a human mind has designed the entire environment deliberately to confuse, except when he chooses to allow the visitor to prevail. There are numerous opportunities for discovery. Sometimes by chance the visitor makes a breakthrough that he had no way of deducing or anticipating, for the simple reason that the designer deliberately concealed the experience lying in wait to be discovered, all as part of the fun.

Maze designers need to be responsive to their audience, and constantly learn and discover by observing how people behave when finding new maze challenges. For example, in cornfield mazes when we introduced flags to be carried by visitors we experimented with how they were handed out. Initially, all visitors were given flags, to engender a sense of belonging to a group (essential in mazes on this scale!). However, children still tended to rush off in all directions. The insight came when we limited one flag to each family, so that the 'standard bearer' formed the focal point of the group. The group dynamic changed dramatically; children vied with each other to take turns carrying the flag, looked to a grown-up to decide when the changeover should happen, and meanwhile were content to follow the flag rather than break away. This encouraged families to stay together throughout their visit, noticing each others' behaviour, engaging, bonding, and ensuring that nobody got lost!

Of course, like a movie production or architectural project, there remain innumerable unseen practical issues: the specification, budget, cash-flow, planning permission and project timescale, covering everything from getting plants to grow in particular soils and micro-climates to the timely arrival of mirror maze pieces within customs-cleared containers at a far-flung port.

But these are practical construction issues, rather than the essence of the maze puzzle or visitor experience, which is what concerns us here. So how should we assess the qualities of the ultimate puzzle maze? Perhaps we should judge it like ice skating: up to six points each for Technical Merit and Artistic Impression!

221

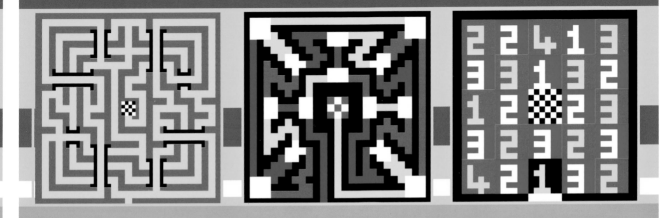

QUICK MAZES

The essential maze experience remains compelling whatever mazes are made of. One significant modern development has been Quick Mazes, where the solving time and physical size are reduced, and yet the puzzle 'variety' is dramatically increased. Mazes created on internet websites and computer software allow players to explore realms that may be physically impossible to construct – for example, the Eight-Page One-Way Drop-Through Multi-Layer Maze on p. 248.

PUZZLE MAZES
WITHOUT BARRIERS

Beyond familiar puzzle mazes, there is an entire realm of intriguing ideas and variations! Physical barriers are often replaced with rules – colour, numbers or specific movements – to create new dimensions.

A range of portable quick mazes at set-up in front of Cathedrals and at the waterfront at Old Portsmouth.

We love to master new challenges, and the mazes here provide not just new network patterns, but also new ways of moving, new things to move about, new forms of pathway, and new rules to discover. I coined the phrase 'Six Minute' mazes to describe short-timescale mazes. Some are mazes with rules, where half the fun is discovering how to move. Some are geometric puzzles where the right angle is banned. Some provide an escape from numbers, using instead the beauty of shapes, proportions, colours and sizes.

Though such mazes work well on paper, since the 1980s I have also been creating portable versions using interlocking plastic tiles. Visitors solve tile and paving mazes by actually walking on the design. The challenge is to design concise puzzles, since most people enjoy them best if solved within a few minutes. Often the shortest solution only involves 8, 10, 12 or 15 moves – but which moves, and in which order?

We begin with two-dimensional puzzle mazes, which do not differ substantially from paving mazes; then 'bridges' are introduced to make the designs three-dimensional. Headlong and One-Way mazes build on the rules of some of the path-in-grass mazes seen in the last section. Colour mazes develop the concept of 'multi-state mazes', where your options at the same point in space vary, depending on how you approach it. New rules are introduced, and even new ways of moving, in the case of Jumping Mazes. Quick Mazes bring out playful, recreational aspects of mathematics, and offer great family experiences.

TWO-DIMENSIONAL MAZES

These two simple two-dimensional puzzle mazes start your quest of solving Quick Mazes. Simply follow the yellow paths and make decisions at the path junctions, as you work from the entrance of the maze to your goal – the red square at the centre. Once people used to think that the 'Hand-on-Wall Rule' would always solve puzzle mazes. To apply this rule, imagine the walls are tall, and you must always keep your left hand on the left-hand wall, following it in and out as you go. Very quickly, you will realize that this method will not solve either of these two-dimensional mazes. First try the easier of them (above) and then the harder one (below).

THREE-DIMENSIONAL MAZES

Bridges allow us to add an extra dimension to achieve a three-dimensional network. There are the same start and goal points as in the two-dimensional mazes – you move from the start at the bottom of each maze to the chequered goal square at the centre – but this time you have to hold in your mind both the underlying network of paths and the connections made by the bridges. Start with the smallest version (opposite, top left) and see how you get better at visualizing each three-dimensional layout as you progress. Incidentally, in each maze the bridges possess a four-fold rotational symmetry; this aspect isn't crucial to the puzzles, but it's just an extra flourish we like to include in our designs. By the time you've cracked the fourth maze with twenty bridges, you'll be a three-dimensional maze master!

TWO-COLOUR MAZES

What if the choices in a maze didn't simply relate to the junctions, but to the paths themselves? What if the path had significance, and that the type of path dictated whether you could go down it or not? Both of the maze designs shown here are based on two colours, with either an entire path being marked with colour between junctions (the Star 21 Maze, opposite) or a coloured square within the length of a path (the 'Hot & Cold' mazes, below). In both mazes you have to go from the start at the bottom to the goal at the centre and to change colour alternately on each path you go down. With the Hot and Cold Mazes, you must continue your direction through the coloured space; turning back is not allowed.

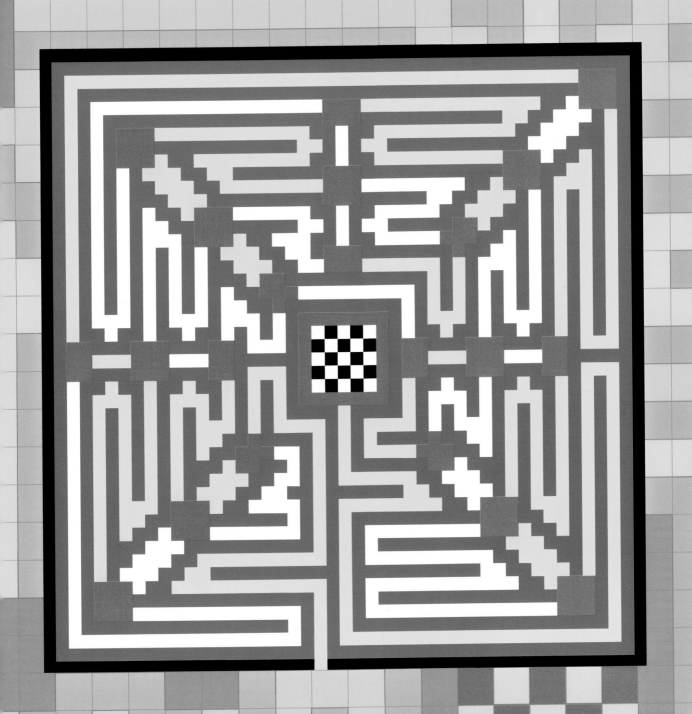

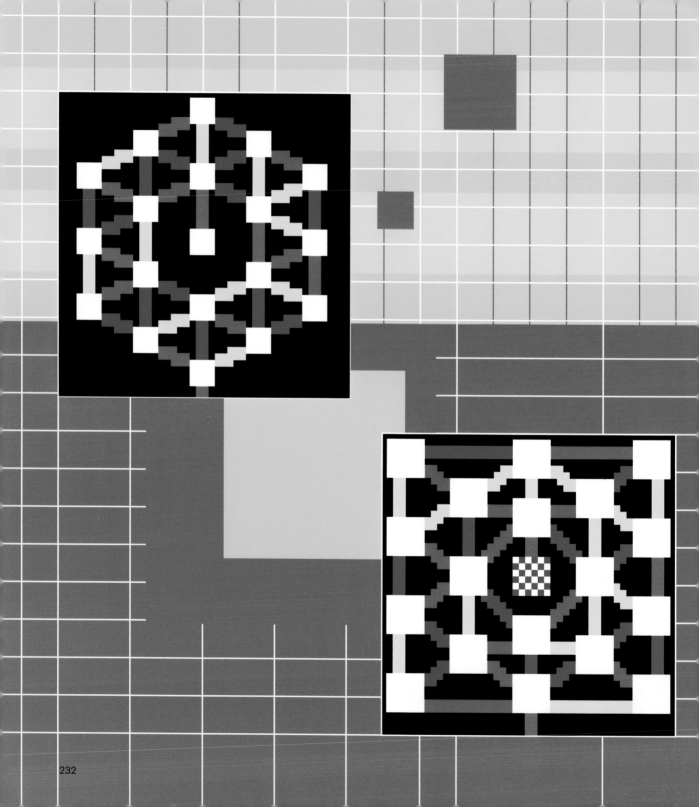

THREE-COLOUR MAZES

These mazes are based on three-colour alternation – another mindset to master. On this page, the two 'Traffic Lights' mazes are solved using the sequence Red-Yellow-Green repeatedly. The 'Snowflake maze' (opposite, top left) is solved using the sequence Red-Blue-Yellow repeatedly. A greater challenge is presented by the 'Mathematica maze' (opposite, bottom right), which can be solved in two different colour sequences: Red-Blue-Yellow and Red-Yellow-Blue, both of which are difficult and take completely different routes around the maze. This design, built in coloured brick paving outside the Mathematics Building at Leicester University in England, was created in memory of my sister Victoria who was a lecturer at the University.

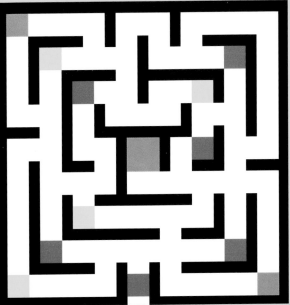

FOUR-COLOUR MAZES

Now, can you handle four colours in a strictly repeated sequence? With the Rainbow Maze (above), whenever you reach a junction square, you have to change path colour in the repeated sequence Red-Blue-Yellow-Green. You will find that certain junctions have to be used as many as four times. Start at the bottom and aim for the goal at the centre. The design of the Giant's Bridge Maze (opposite) was first featured in *Scientific American* magazine in 1984; it is based on the topological fact that 7 is the maximum number of points on a doughnut-shaped torus ring, where every point is connected to every other by lines drawn on its surface. The use of one giant bridge on a plane surface simulates the linked points which would occur on a torus – to achieve the connections, some paths pass both over and under the bridge between junctions. The start point is the square at the bottom left, the goal is the square at the centre of the top row – you must change path colour in the repeated sequence Red-Blue-Yellow-Green.

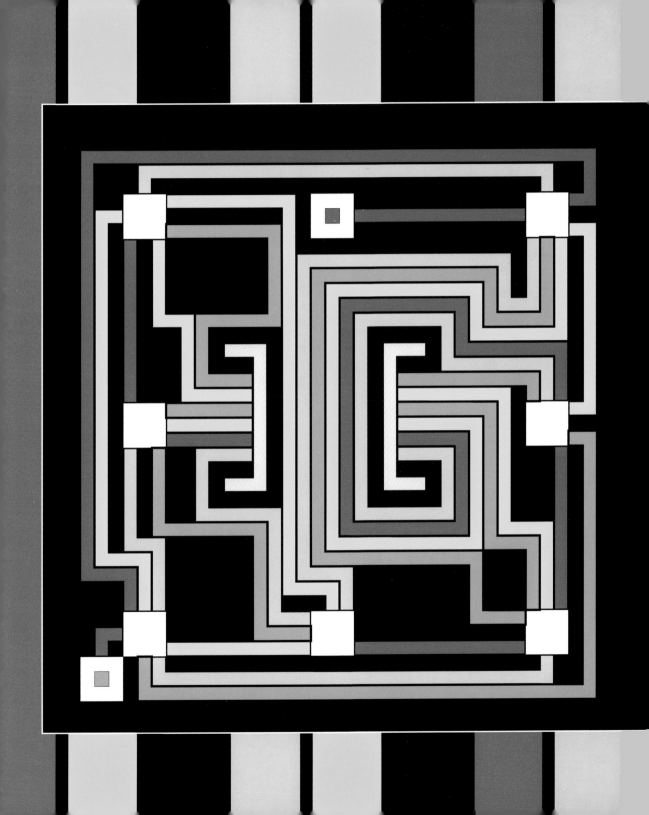

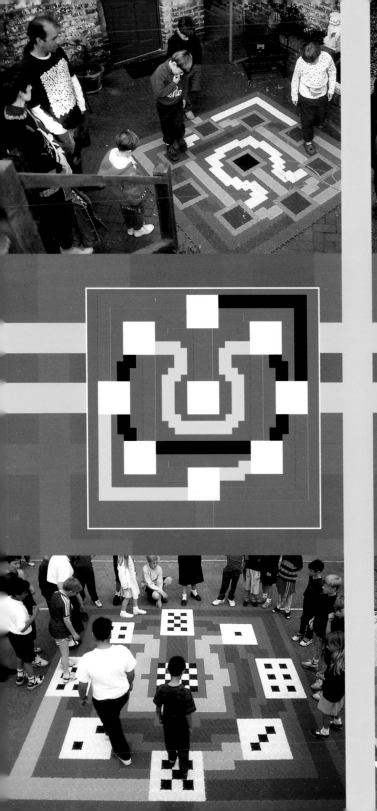

'ANY COLOUR' MAZES

These mazes require you to change path colour to any other colour, whenever you reach a junction. For example, if you enter a junction square from a Red path, you may depart on a Blue path or a Yellow path, but not on another Red path. Mathematically this is more complex than two-colour, three-colour or four-colour sequential mazes. Sometimes you have to return to the same square a second time, in order to depart on the true path colour that you wished to use

all along, but could not take your first time through. In terms of complexity, there are 3 sets of outcomes from each junction, so even our smallest example, the Circle 8 Maze, has 24 sets of outcomes – compared with 8 sets of choices in the famous hedge maze at Hampton Court Palace. The 'Circle 8' and 'Circle 12' puzzles are opposite, whilst the 'Lattice 12' maze is above. Each puzzle has its starting path at the bottom and its goal at the centre.

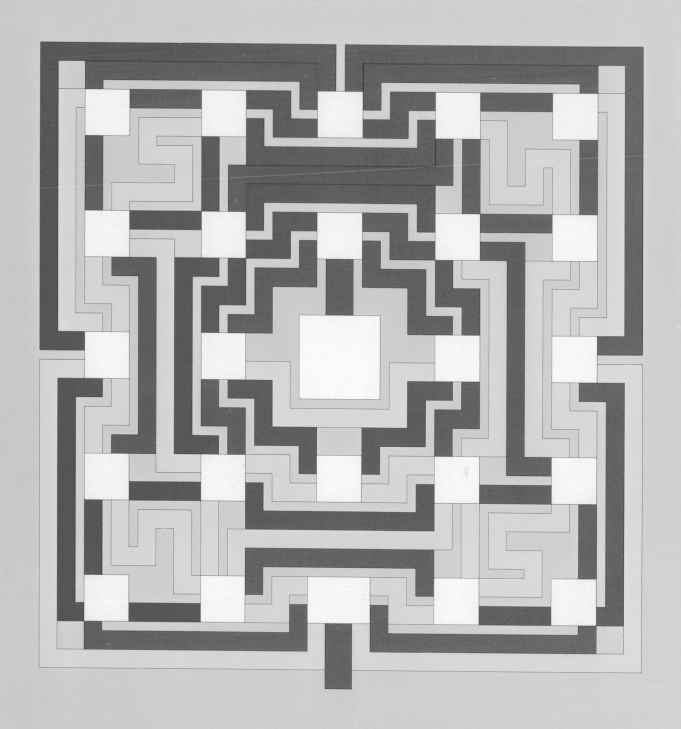

238

ALPHABET SOUP AND COLOUR STAR MAZES

The 'Star 14' and 'Star 17' mazes below are variations on the 'any colour' mazes we have just seen – each time you leave a junction, you must change from the colour of your previous path. The 'Alphabet Soup' maze (opposite) was originally published in *Scientific American* magazine in 1984. At each junction, you have to change path colour. The twist this time is that the maze has a double ring of defences in its junctions, which has only one point where you can enter the inner part of the design. It is all too easy to find

yourself forced back to the entrance of the maze. When designing this maze, I had the mental image of sitting on a large smooth roundabout: unless you are at its precise centre, the faster it spins, the more likely centrifugal force will throw you off. Our mazes often have incongruous names. Here the two smaller mazes have 14 and 17 junction cells respectively, laid out in a star formation. 'Alphabet Soup' can contain 25 letters of the alphabet, and thus be customized so that its solution creates a special 9-letter anagram to solve.

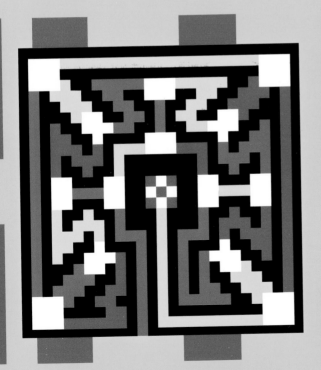

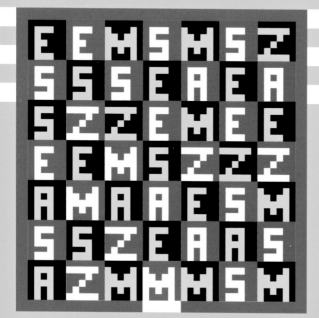
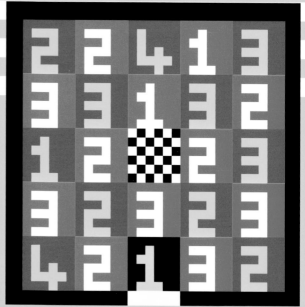

JUMPING MAZES

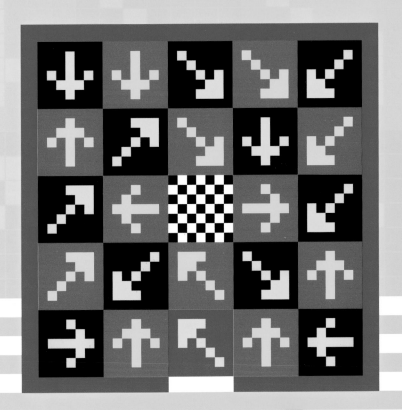

It is commonly believed that all puzzle mazes must have a start, pathways, barriers, decision points and a goal. This is not true of Jumping Mazes! Jumping Mazes have their decision points laid out as a grid of squares, with the connecting paths being hops through the air. In each of the maze designs shown here, start from the centre square of the bottom row, with your goal being the central square. In the Arrow Maze (above), the arrow in each cell dictates your direction of travel, but you choose the distance to jump in a straight line. In the Number Maze (shown left), the rule is reversed. The number on each square dictates the how many squares you must travel on the next jump, but you can decide which direction to take. No diagonal jumps are allowed. The toughest of the three is the Knight's Maze (far left). You simultaneously make each move like a knight in chess (two squares forward and one to the side), while repeatedly spelling out the word M-A-Z-E-S- as you go. Your final jump brings you to the letter S at the centre. With its 49 junction squares and its 5-letter sequence, it was quite a design challenge to ensure that there were no Black Holes in the design where you could get stuck and be unable to continue.

ONE-WAY MAZES

Here are three different kinds of One-Way Maze, where you must keep going forwards. In each there is a special rule which tells you when you may make choices. In each One-Way Maze, start by moving forwards up the path at the bottom of each design; in each instance your goal is the target circle at the end of a path. In the two Jammed Tractor Mazes (above), imagine you are a farmer driving your tractor. Suddenly the steering becomes jammed so

that you can only drive straight ahead or steer left. How can you possibly get home? (Exceptionally, in Jammed Tractor Mazes you sometimes get stuck in a corner – if this happens, abandon your attempt and start again.) In the two Headlong Mazes (opposite page, above), you must always keep going straight ahead, or as they say, forwards 'headlong'. If the path curves round a corner, you must follow it. The only time you get a choice is when you reach a wall blocking your path; then and only then may you choose to turn left or right. It is no consolation that there are maze paths left and right everywhere – if you have not hit a wall headlong, these are forbidden turnings. The fifth design is a Starpoint Maze (right), where you must always go straight ahead unless you come across a Star or hit a wall. At these, you must turn left or right; you are not allowed to continue straight ahead. You must follow curved paths.

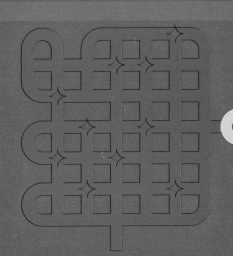

1

2

3

BIZARRE BIPLANE MAZES

These square 'Bizarre Biplane' Mazes are another variation of One-Way Mazes. They are based on the premise that early aircraft were notoriously unable to make tight turns. When you are allowed to make a decision, you can only go straight ahead or turn 90 degrees to the left or right; no diagonal moves are allowed. Thus you cannot perform U-turns, and a 180-degree turn takes a minimum of two moves. Black squares are mountains, which must be flown around. On this page: (1) move using distances of 1-2-1-2- repeatedly; (2) move using distances of 1-2-3- repeatedly; (3) move using distances of 1-3-1-3- repeatedly. On the opposite page: (4) move using distances of 1-2-3-4- repeatedly; (5) move using distances of 1-2-3- repeatedly; (6) move using distances of 1-2-3-4- repeatedly; (7) move using distances of 1-2-3-4- repeatedly; (8) move using distances of 1-2-3-4- repeatedly; (9) move using distances of 1-2-3-4-5- repeatedly.

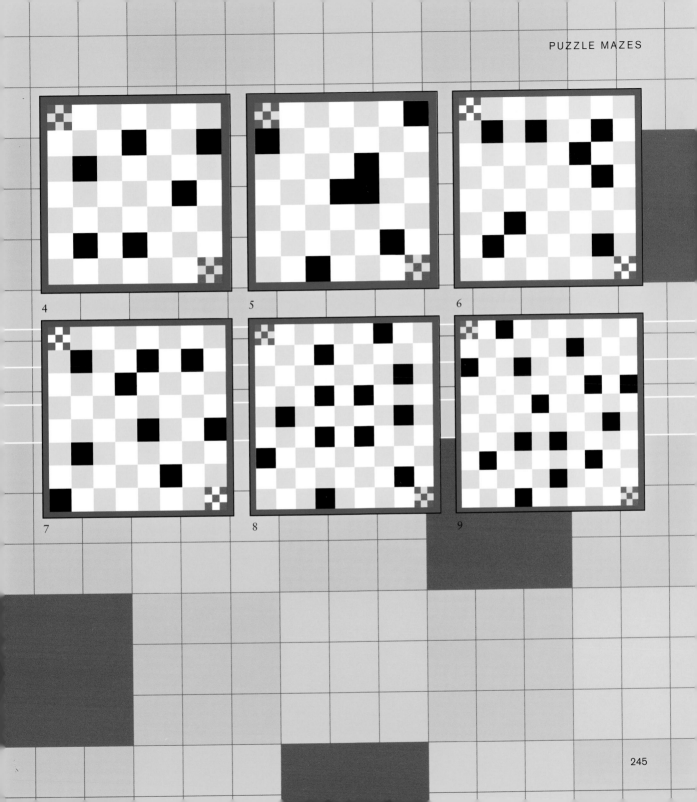

4

5

6

7

8

9

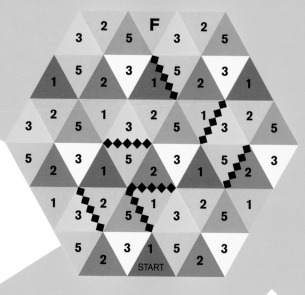

10

11

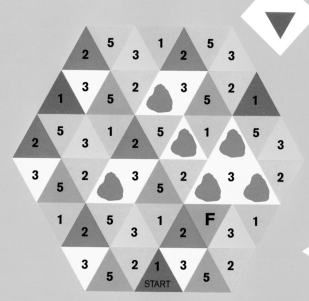

12

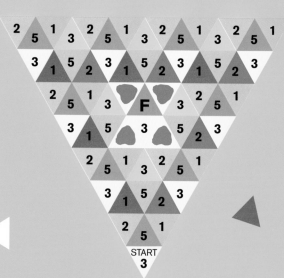

13

TRIANGULAR AND HEXAGONAL BIZARRE BIPLANE MAZES

These triangular and hexagonal 'Bizarre Biplane' Mazes develop the ideas seen on the previous spread, and are yet another variation on One-Way Mazes. You must move given distances in straight lines, according to the number in the cell where you happen to be. From the Start, finish precisely in the cell marked F. At the end of each jump, you can only go straight ahead or turn 60 degrees to the left or right. Thus you cannot perform 120 degree turns; and a 180 degree turn takes a minimum of three moves. Mountains are indicated in black, with thin 'walls' of black diamonds (10) or solid hexagonal cells (11). Finally, Biplanes are not allowed to start or end any jump on a lake; mazes 12, 13 and 14 contain numerous lakes. In case you're struggling with these mazes, take a look at www.mazepuzzle.com

14

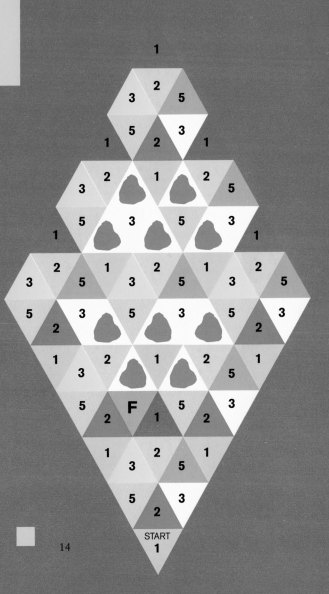

ADRIAN FISHER'S 3D MAZE CHALLENGE

Are you ready for the Ultimate 3D maze challenge? Are you ready to take on a maze that, if it were built to human scale, would shatter the Guinness World Record for the biggest maze by path length?

Do not be daunted by the size of this Eight Page One-Way Drop-Through Multi-Layer Maze! Although the maze is undeniably complex, the rules are actually fairly simple:

1. Follow the maze paths from Start to Finish.

2. Paths weave over and under each other, using bridges and underpasses.

3. Travel from page to page, turning the pages over as necessary to trace your route.

4. You can travel from one outer page to another, as long as the triangles of both pages match each other's colour (yellow to yellow, and blue to blue). Line up the pages carefully, so you connect accurately with the opposite path.

5. Whenever you reach a circular hole, turn the page until it is aligned above a lower page; you will find it is above a Junction. DROP THROUGH THE HOLE, fold the upper page aside, and continue your maze journey from this new Junction.

6. Your challenge is to reach the Finish!

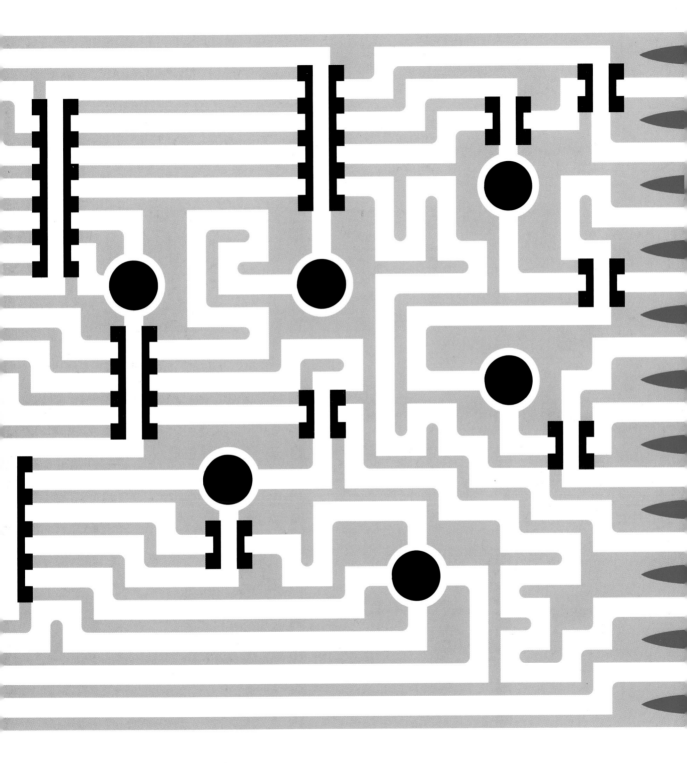

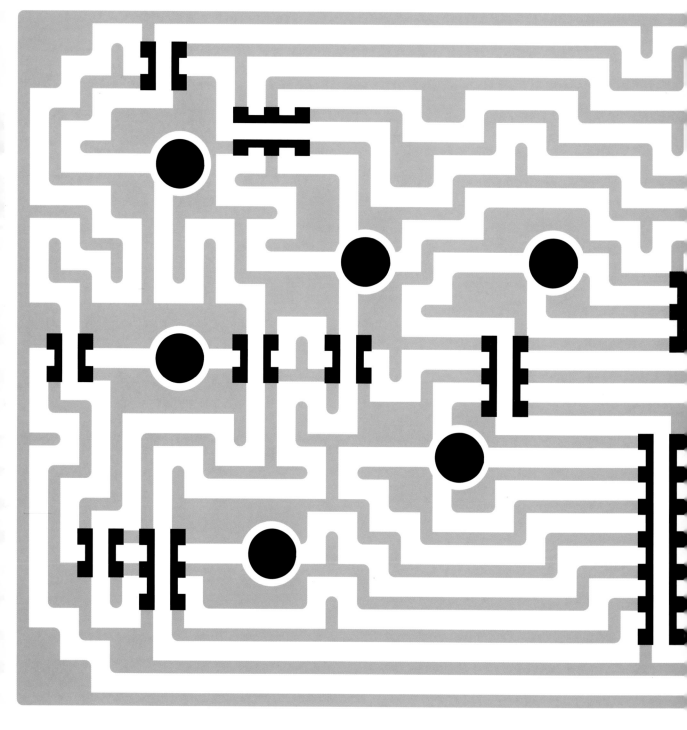

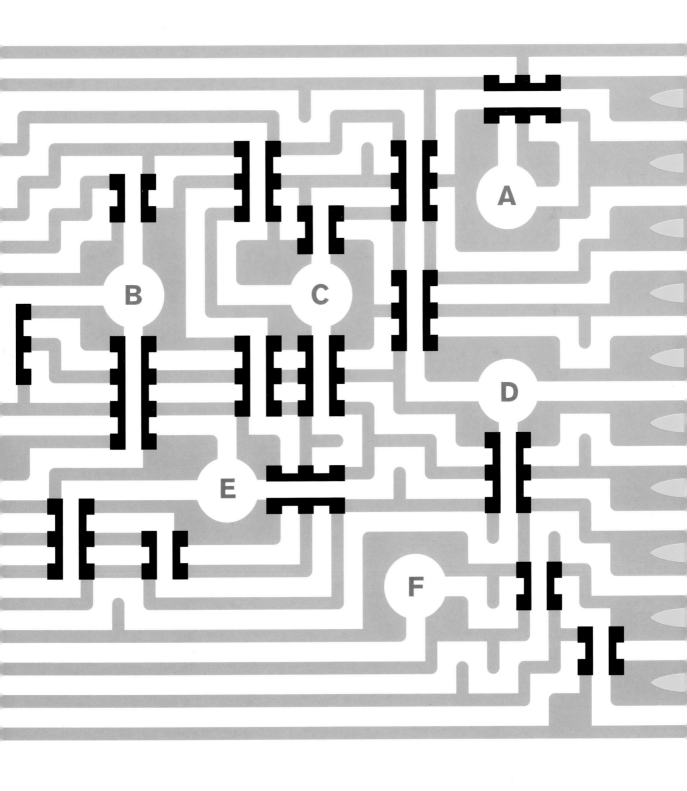

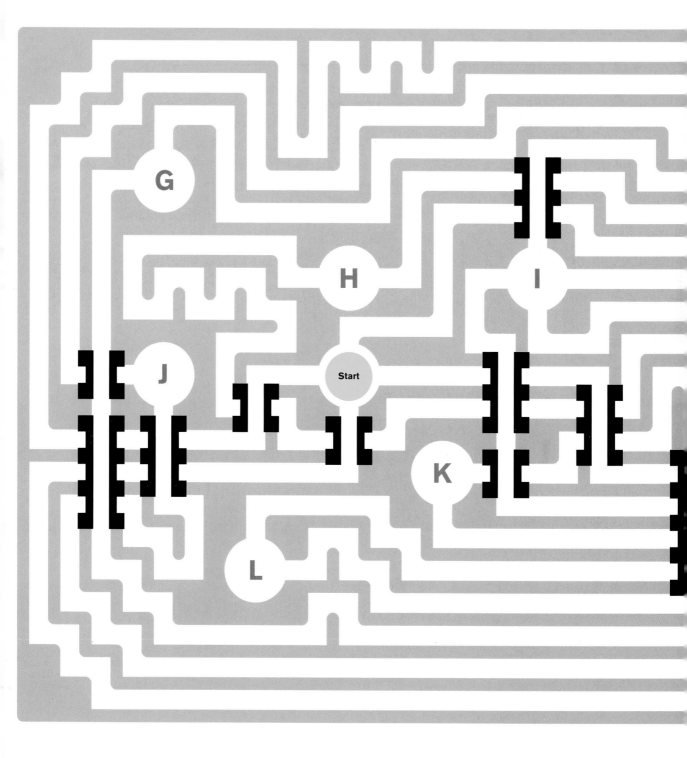

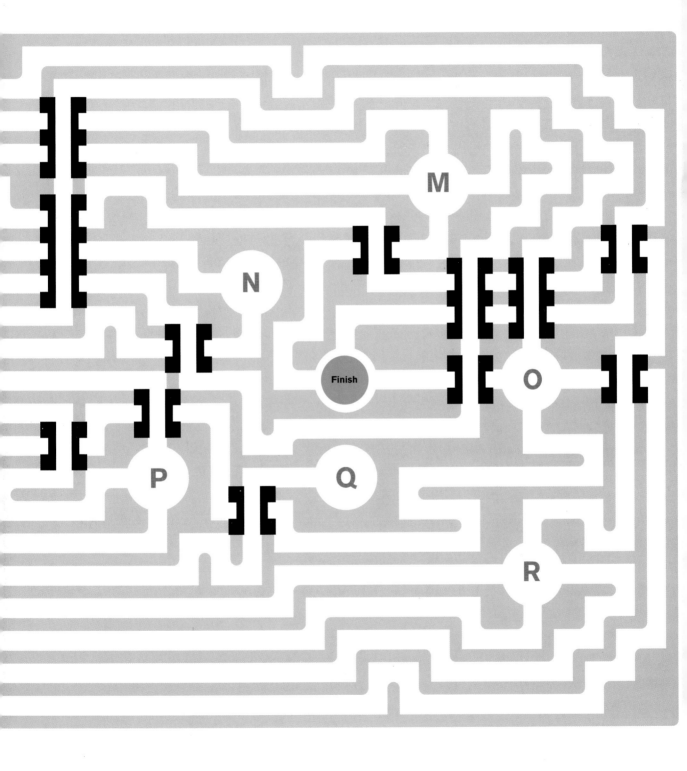

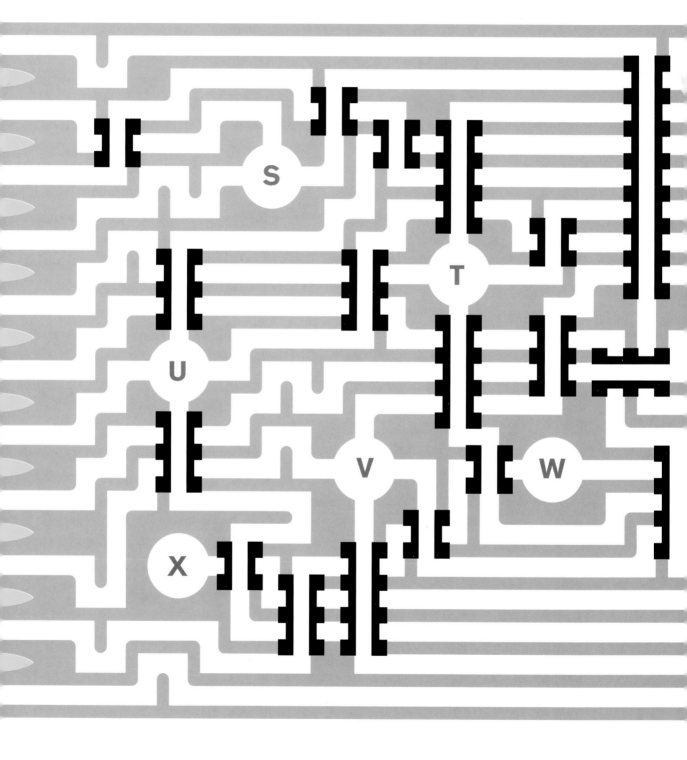

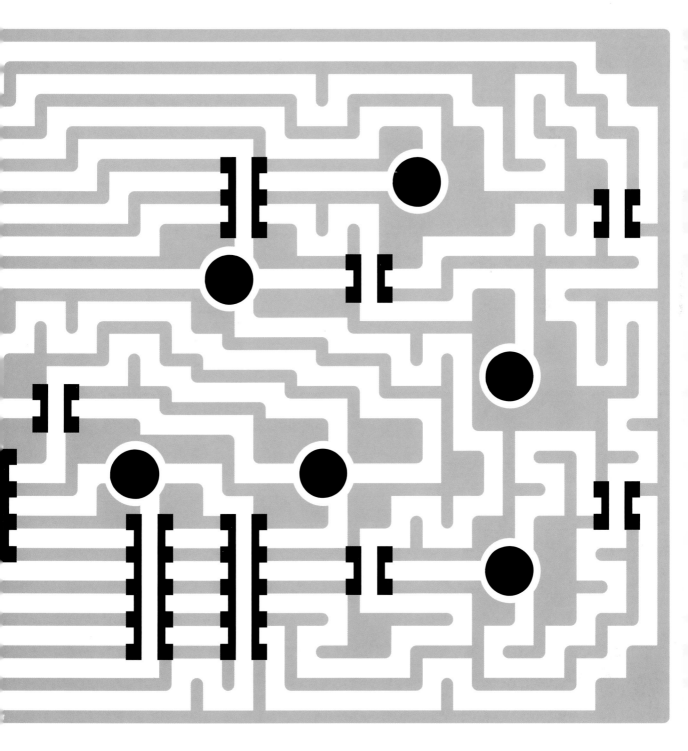

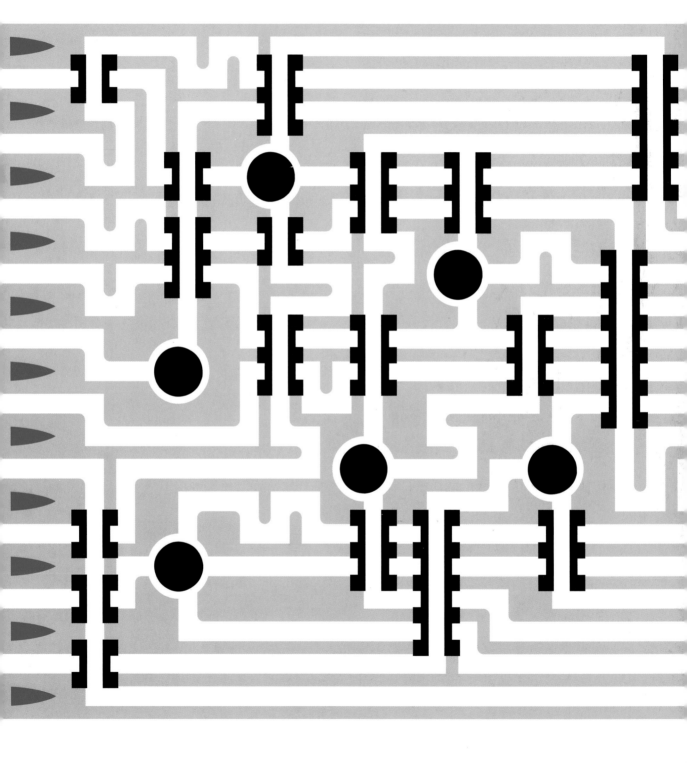

GLOSSARY OF MAZE TERMS

Mazes have distinctive aspects that cry out for specific terminology. Some terms date back centuries, but many have only been coined in the past few years, in response to new situations.

ADJUSTABLE MAZE – A maze whose barriers can be adjusted from day to day, or session to session, by the use of MAZE GATES.

BLACK HOLE – A place in a COLOUR MAZE or One-Way Maze which one can get into, but not out of. The finest maze designs have no Black Holes. The opposite of a WHITE HOLE.

CAERDROIA – Welsh word. Usually used for a unicursal turf labyrinth.

COLOUR MAZE – A Quick Maze where path colour is a crucial part of the puzzle.

CONDITIONAL DIRECTION MAZE – A maze with one-way passages.

CONDITIONAL MOVEMENT MAZE – A maze where each move depends on the previous move. The choice at each junction depends on how you approach it. A COLOUR MAZE is an example of a conditional movement maze.

DOUBLE-DECKER BRIDGE – A splendid bit of exuberance, since any three-dimensional network can be achieved using bridges just one deck high. Great fun!

FOAMING FOUNTAIN GATES – A keynote feature invented by Adrian Fisher Mazes, and pioneered in various puzzle mazes including Holywell Bay Fun Park, Blackpool Pleasure Beach, Edinburgh Zoo, Legoland Windsor and Three Lands Point, Netherlands.

FORCED PATH – A maze situation which only has one way forward. Encountered in COLOUR MAZES.

FRYING PAN – A feature within a THREE-DIMENSIONAL MAZE, whereby the perimeter of an area cannot be penetrated. The way out is by a bridge over the perimeter, or through a tunnel under it

GOAL – The objective of the maze. Nearly all mazes have a goal, and usually only one.

HAND-ON-WALL METHOD – A method which solves SIMPLY-CONNECTED mazes, but is defeated by MULTIPLY-CONNECTED mazes.

INTERACTIVE MAZE – A maze whose design changes in response to actions of visitors.

INTERNAL ROTATIONAL SYMMETRY – A hallmark of all Classical, Roman and Medieval Christian LABYRINTHS. If the design is cut from the entrance to the goal and 'folded out' to form a rectangle, then the resulting array of parallel paths should possess rotational symmetry.

ISLAND – A continuously linked piece of hedging (or other barrier) within a maze not linked to the perimeter hedge. Islands only occur in multicursal mazes.

LABYRINTH – From an unknown archaic source, and adopted in most languages from the Greek word Labyrinthos, referring to the legendary maze constructed for King Minos by Daedalus to house the Minotaur. Although used interchangeably with maze, labyrinth tends to apply to mineral, and maze to vegetal networks. There are three essential forms of labyrinth: CLASSICAL (the archetypal design, found in many parts of the world, generally with seven rings of paths, with all changes of path direction occurring on the central axis between the entrance and the goal); ROMAN (which typically has four quadrants, with an internal logic of the Classical design repeated four times); and MEDIEVAL CHRISTIAN (unicursal, with paths doubling back on all four axes, thus producing a cruciform image – typically with eleven rings of paths, although seven and fifteen are also found). In addition there are processional labyrinths, similar to a UNICURSAL Classical labyrinth, but with an additional short exit from the goal, making it possible for a procession of people to pass through the labyrinth without congestion at the goal.

MARKERS – Leaving markers in a maze to record one's progress is considered very bad form.

MAZE GATES – Can be unlocked, moved and re-locked at regular intervals. In a puzzle maze, the movement of a single barrier changes the logic of the entire maze; where a number of Maze Gates are included within a maze, there can be many different puzzle combinations. Examples can be found at Escot Park Hedge Maze, Devon, and Castle Loucen in the Czech Republic.

MULTIPLY-CONNECTED – A multicursal maze with forking paths, some of which link up with each other further on in the maze; thus it will have one or more islands within it. A multiply-connected maze must have its GOAL located on an ISLAND.

NODE – A junction or decision point, where three or more paths meet.

NOTATION – Graph Theory, the study of networks, offers a form of notation for the most complex of mazes. Any maze can be represented by a matrix. This form of analysis can be applied to complex mazes which are not readily solvable by sight.

QUICK EXIT – In a puzzle maze, a quick exit avoids doubling the time of the visit, after reaching the goal. If the maze is MULTIPLY-CONNECTED, this can only be preserved if the quick exit crosses over or under the perimeter path, by bridge or tunnel.

ROTATING HEDGE – A feature invented by Adrian Fisher, and pioneered in a private maze in Dorset, England. A 3-metre (10-foot) length of hedge is mounted on a turntable, which allows the hedge to rotate 90 degrees, thus completely changing the puzzle design of the maze.

SIMPLY-CONNECTED – A multicursal maze with a series of dead-ends leading off the one true path. Although one or more islands may be present, the goal is attached albeit tenuously to the perimeter.

SLIDING-SEAT-AND-HEDGE – A keynote feature invented by Adrian Fisher, and being pioneered in private hedge mazes in Southern England. What seems to be an innocent garden seat set into a hedge recess turns out to be a seat that can slide backwards 5 metres (15 feet) along a light railway track – complete with bushes behind in containers mounted on a four-wheel railway truck.

SPAN – A unit of measure, for comparison between mazes of different scales. In a barrier maze, a span is measured from the centre-line of one barrier to the centre-line of the next. In a turf or pavement maze, a span may be measured from the centre-line of one path to the centre-line of the next.

SPAN-SQUARE – An imaginary square measured along the length of a path, based on the maze's span unit. The number of span squares containing nodes can be expressed as a percentage of the total number of span squares in the maze. This is one useful way to evaluate the difficulty of a maze.

STRAIGHT-LINE DIAGRAM – A way of summarizing the topology of a maze, while eliminating non-essential detail. The entrance, a triangle, is connected to the goal, a circle, by the shortest solution, a straight line, Incidental paths fork off each side of the line.

THREE-DIMENSIONAL MAZE – A maze whose paths cross over and under each other.

TIME-DIMENSIONAL MAZE – A maze whose barriers can change from moment to moment while visitors are inside it. Time provides an extra dimension, but only forwards.

UNDERGROUND EXIT TUNNEL – A rare but splendid maze feature. The very few examples worldwide include Leeds Castle Hedge Maze, Kent and Sigurta Gardens Hedge Maze, Italy.

UNICURSAL – 'Single-pathed', a maze with no junctions or decision points (NODES). From the GOAL, the visitor has to retrace his path entirely to return to the entrance.

WHITE HOLE – A maze situation which one cannot get into, but if one was in it, one could get out of it. It's an ingenious design technique used to thwart players who try and work out a maze design backwards, for whom the maze designer has no sympathy. Can occur in COLOUR MAZES. The opposite of a BLACK HOLE.

RECORD-BREAKING MAZES

World Records are the lifeblood of maze-making – here are the biggest, oldest, and most difficult mazes! The rules for the world's largest mazes, as applied by the Guinness Book of World Records, stipulate that paths and barriers should be of appropriately compact dimensions for any given method of construction. Valid hedges should be typically 1 to 2 metres (3 to 6 feet) thick; valid corn maze barriers should be typically 3 to 5 metres (8 to 15 feet) thick. Excessively large goal areas are not to be included.

LARGEST AREA, PERMANENT MAZE
1891 – Castle Ruurlo, Netherlands
   approx. area 8,571 sq. m. (92,400 sq. ft) – though not strictly valid, since its 5-metre (15-foot) paths are so wide.
1978 – Longleat House, Wiltshire, England: 6,169 sq. m. (66,403 sq. ft)
1998 – Pineapple Maze, Dole Plantation, Hawaii: not including the central goal, 6,957 sq. m. (75,000 sq. ft)

LONGEST PATH LENGTH, PERMANENT MAZE
1891 – Castle Ruurlo, Netherlands: 1,563 m. (5,133 ft)
1978 – Longleat House, Wiltshire, England: 3,084 m. (10,125 ft)

LARGEST AREA, SEASONAL MAZE
1993 – Lebanon Valley College, Pennsylvania, USA; 11,706 sq. m. (126,000 sq. ft / 2.893 acres); designed by Adrian Fisher

1995 – Shippensburg, PA, USA; 16,000 sq. m. (172,225 sq. ft / 3.954 acres); designed by Adrian Fisher

1996 – Dearborn, MI, USA; 24,507 sq. m. (263,790 sq. ft / 6.056 acres); designed by Adrian Fisher

1997 – Millets Farm Centre, Oxfordshire, England; 30,716 sq. m. (330,620 sq. ft / 7.59 acres); designed by Adrian Fisher

2002 – Stewarts Garden Centre, Dorset, England; 59,177 sq. m. (636,978 sq. ft /14.623 acres); designed by Adrian Fisher

2003 – Stewarts Garden Centre, Dorset, England: 68,271 sq. m. (736,208 sq. ft / 16.901 acres); designed by Adrian Fisher

LONGEST PATH, SEASONAL MAZE

1993 – Lebanon Valley College, Pennsylvania, USA; 2,414 m. (7,920 ft / 1.5 miles) of paths; designed by Adrian Fisher

1995 – Shippensburg, Pennsylvania, USA; 3,267 m. (10,718 ft / 2.03 miles) of paths; designed by Adrian Fisher

1996 – Dearborn, Michigan, USA; 4,844 m. (15,893 ft / 3.01 miles) of paths; designed by Adrian Fisher

1997 – Millets Farm Centre, Oxfordshire, England; 6,003 m. (19,694 ft / 3.73 miles) of paths; designed by Adrian Fisher

2002 – Stewarts Garden Centre, Dorset, England; 11,114 m. (36,464 ft / 6.906 miles) of paths; designed by Adrian Fisher

2003 – Stewarts Garden Centre, Dorset, England; 14,227 m. (46,675 ft /8.84 miles) of paths; designed by Adrian Fisher

LARGEST MIRROR MAZE

The World Records for both largest area of mirrored cells, and longest path length through the mirrored cells, are held by the same maze:

1994 – Mirror Maze, Peaugres Safari Park, France: net area (visitable space of mirrored cells): 115 sq. m.; gross area (including 'gag chambers', tableaux, etc.): 124 sq. m.; Path length: 63 m.; designed by Adrian Fisher

WORLD'S FIRST...

Cornfield Maize Maze – Lebanon Valley College, Pennsylvania, USA, 1993, designed by Adrian Fisher

Vertical Water Maze – Jersey Water Maze, 1997, designed by Adrian Fisher

Path-in-Grass Maze – 1981, Greys Court, Oxfordshire, England. Designed by Randoll Coate and Adrian Fisher

Mirror Maze – Constantinople, Turkey, 1889

Hedge Maze (with head-high hedges and tight puzzle) – Nonsuch Palace, Surrery, England, 1599

Hedge Maze with islands – Chevening House, Kent, England, planted c. 1820

Hedge Maze with bridges – Longleat House, Wiltshire, 1978

Hedge Maze with a tunnel – Leeds Castle, Kent, 1988

WORLD'S OLDEST SURVIVING...

Mosaic Labyrinth – c. 165 BC, opus signinum pavement, Mieza, Greece

Carved Labyrinth – c. 2,000 BC, petroglyphs, Pontevedra and Galicia, Spain

Stone Pavement Labyrinth – 1200–1210, Chartres Cathedral, France

Hedge Maze – 1690, Hampton Court Palace, England

Turf Maze – 1642, The Rad, Eilenreide Forest, Hannover, Germany

Mirror Maze – 1891, Petrin Mirror Maze, Petrin Hill, Prague, Czech Republic

THE WORLD'S BEST MAZES

A selection of the mazes that every enthusiast must visit at least once in their life, arranged by country.

AUSTRALIA
Ashcombe Hedge Maze, Victoria; www.ashcombemaze.com.au
Bellingham Hedge Maze, Queensland; www.bellmaze.com
Arthur's Seat Hedge Maze, Victoria;

www.arthursseatmaze.com.au
Hedgend Hedge Maze, Healsville, Victoria; www.hedgend.com.au

AUSTRIA
Hedge Maze, Schönbrunn Palace,

Vienna; www.schoenbrunn.at
Kristallwelten Hedge Maze, Wattens; www.swarovski.com/ kristallwelten

BELGIUM
Château de Beloeil Hedge Maze; www.beloeil.be
Hedge Maze, Château de Loppem
Van Burren Museum Hedge Maze, Brussels

CANADA
Saunder's Farm, Ontario;
www.saundersfarm.com
Vandusen Gardens Maze,
Vancouver, B. C.

CZECH REPUBLIC
Petrin Hill Mirror Maze, Prague
Castle Loucen Hedge Maze;
www.loucen.cz

DENMARK
'Labyrinthia' collection of mazes,
Rodelund; www.labyrinthia.dk
Egeskov Hedge Maze, Fyn Island
www.egeskov.dk

ENGLAND
Hampton Court Palace
www.hrp.org.uk
Leeds Castle Hedge Maze;
www.leeds-castle.co.uk
Longleat House Hedge and Mirror
Mazes; www.longleat.co.uk
Blenheim Palace Hedge Maze;
www.blenheimpalace.com
Chatsworth House Hedge Maze;
www.chatsworth.org
Legoland Hedge Maze, Windsor;
www.legoland.co.uk
Chinese Puzzle Maze, Blackpool
Pleasure Beach;
www.blackpoolpleasurebeach.co.uk
Wookey Hole Mirror Maze;
www.wookey.co.uk
Mirror Mazes, London and York
Dungeons;
www.thedungeons.com
Hever Castle Hedge and Water
Mazes; www.hever-castle.co.uk
Jersey Water Maze, St Helier
Tudor Rose Maze, Kentwell Hall;
www.kentwell.co.uk
Archbishop's Maze, Greys Court;
www.nationaltrust.org.uk

Beazer Gardens Path-in-Grass
Maze, Bath, Avon

Seasonal corn mazes include:
Tulleys Farm, West Sussex;
www.tulleysfarm.com
Millets Farm, Oxfordshire;
www.milletsfarmcentre.com
Rodden Farm, Dorset;
www.greatdorsetmaizemaze.co.uk

FRANCE
Château de Thoiry Hedge Maze,
Thoiry, Yvelines;
www.zoo-thoiry.com
Peaugres Safari Park Mirror Maze,
Annonay, nr Lyons;
www.safari-peaugres.com
Château de Villandry Hedge Maze,
Indre-et-Loire;
www.chateauvillandry.com
Le Labyrinthe aux Oiseaux,
Chateau d'Yvoire
Wonderland Hedge Maze,
Eurodisney;
www.disneylandparis.com

GERMANY
Hamburg Dungeon Mirror Maze;
www.thedungeons.com
Hedge Maze, Herrenhausen;
Gardens, Hannover
www.hannover.de/herrenhausen
Kleinwelka Hedge Maze;
www.irrgarten-kleinwelka.de

INDIA
Mirror Maze, Prasad IMAX
Theatre, Hyderabad
www.prasadz.com
Stone-carved labyrinth, Temple of
Hoysalesvara, Halebid, Mysore
Stone-carved labyrinth, Temple of
Kedaresvara, Halebid, Mysore

IRELAND (REPUBLIC OF)
Russborough House Hedge Maze,
Blessington, Co. Wicklow
Dunbrody Abbey Hedge Maze
www.dunbrodyabbey.com

ISRAEL
King's City Mirror Maze, Eilat
www.kingscity.co.il

ITALY
Sigurta Gardens Hedge Maze
www.sigurta.it
Villa Barbarigo Hedge Maze,
Valsanzibio, Venice
www.valsanzibiogiardino.it
Villa Pisani Hedge Maze, Stra
www.villapisani.it
Villa Garzoni Hedge Maze,
Collodi, Tuscany
Palazzo Giusti Hedge Maze, Verona
Hedge Maze, Donna Fugata
Castle, Sicily

NETHERLANDS
Three Lands Point Hedge Maze,
Vaals; www.drielandenpunt.be
Amsterdam Dungeon Mirror Maze
www.thedungeons.com
Amsterdam Forest Hedge Maze

NEW ZEALAND
Wanaka Fence Maze, Wanaka,
South Island
www.puzzlingworld.co.nz
Rotorua Hedge Maze, North Island;

NORTHERN IRELAND
Peace Hedge Maze, Castlewellan
www.peacemaze.com

SCOTLAND
Scone Palace Hedge Maze, Perth;
www.scone-palace.co.uk
Edinburgh Zoo Hedge Maze;
www.edinburghzoo.org.uk
Edinburgh Dungeon Mirror Maze;
www.thedungeons.com

SINGAPORE
Mirror Maze, Singapore Science
Centre; www.science.edu.sg

SOUTH AFRICA
Pavement labyrinth,
Pietermaritzburg Cathedral,
Natal
Soekershof Hedge Maze,
Robertson; www.soekershof.com

SOUTH KOREA
Cheju Island Hedge Maze,
Cheju Island

SPAIN
Hedge Maze, Parc del Laberint
d'Horta, Barcelona
www.bcn.es/parcsijardins/
pa_horta.htm
Hedge Maze, La Granja de San
Ildefonso, Segovia
www.patrimonionacional.es/
granja/granja.htm

SWEDEN
Varmlands Saby Hedge Maze,
Varmlands Province;
www.varmlands-saby.nu
Lisebergparken mirror maze,
Gothenburg

SWITZERLAND
Mirror Maze, Glacier Gardens,
Lucerne;
www.gletschergarten.ch

THAILAND

Ripleys Mirror Maze, Pattaya;
www.ripleysthailand.com

USA

Williamsburg Hedge Maze, Williamsburg, VA;
www.history.org

Amazing Chicago Mirror Maze, Navy Pier,
Chicago, IL; www.amazingchicago.com

Skyline Caverns Mirror Maze, Front Royal, VA;
www.skylinecaverns.com

Noah's Ark Water Park Mirror Maze, Wisconsin
Dells, WI; www.noahsarkwaterpark.com

Coconut Creek Fence Maze, Panama City, FL;
www.coconutcreekfun.com

Norton Museum of Art Paving Maze,
West Palm Beach, FL; www.norton.org

Dole Plantation Hedge Maze, Hawaii, HI;
www.dole-plantation.com

Seasonal corn mazes include:

Davis Megamaze, Stirling, MA;
www.davisfarmland.com

Cherry-Crest Farm, Paradise, PA;
www.cherrycrestfarm.com

Belvedere Plantation, Frederickburg, VA;
www.belvedereplantation.com

FURTHER READING AND RESOURCES

ILLUSTRATED BOOKS

Artress, L., Walking a Sacred Path, New York,
1995

Ashe, G., Labyrinths and Mazes, Wessex Books,
2003

Bord, J., Mazes and Labyrinths of the World,
London, 1976

Candolini, G., Das Geheimnisvolle Labyrinth,
Augsburg, 1999

Coate, R., A. Fisher and G. Burgess, A
Celebration of Mazes, Minotaur Designs,
1986

Fisher, A., Mazes and Labyrinths, Shire
Publications, 2004

—, Mazes and Grottoes, Jarrold Publishing,
2004

—, and G. Gerster, The Art of the Maze,
London, 1990

—, and J. Saward, The British Maze Guide,
1991

—, and H. Loxton, Secrets of the Maze,
London, 1996

Grumbaum, B., and G. C. Shephard, Tilings and
Patterns – an introduction, New York, 1989

Hohmuth, J., Labyrinths and Mazes, Munich,
2003

Kern, H. (ed.), R. Ferre, and J. Saward, Through
the Labyrinth, Munich, 2000

Matthews, W. H., Mazes and Labyrinths – their
history and development, London, 1922

Rouse Ball, W. W., and H. S. M. Coxeter,
Mathematical Recreations and Essays, 1892,
reprinted Dover, 1987

Saward, J., Magical Paths, London, 2002

—, Labyrinths and Mazes, London, 2003

MAZE AND PUZZLE BOOKS

Abbott, B., Mad Mazes, Holbrook, Mass., 1990

—, Supermazes, Rocklin, Calif., 1997

Fisher, A., Mind Bending Maze Puzzles, London,
1999

—, Madcap Mazes, San Francisco, 2005

—, Armchair Puzzlers Mazes, San Francisco,
2005

Hordern, L. E., Sliding Piece Puzzles, Oxford,
1986

Ryan, S., Pencil Puzzlers, New York, 1992

MAZE WEBSITES

www.mazemaker.com – Adrian Fisher's
maze designs of all kinds. Links to
various other of my websites, including:
mirrormaze.com; maizemaze.com;
pavingmaze.com; sixminutemazes.com;
labirinti.com

www.maze-world.com – A catalogue of the
world's mazes.

www.findamaze.com – Choosing mazes to visit
for a day out

www.labyrinthos.net – Labyrinth website of Jeff
Saward and Caerdroia Journal

ONLINE MAZE PUZZLES

www.clickmazes.com – website of Andrea
Gilbert, also featuring Oskar van Deventer

www.logicmazes.com – website of Robert Abbott

www.mathpuzzle.com – website of Ed Pegg Jr.

www.mazepuzzle.com – website of Adrian
Fisher's Maze Puzzles

www.navigatimaze.com – website of Adrian
Fisher's NAVIGATI puzzles

www.puzzlebeast.com – website of James
Stephens, also featuring Oskar van Deventer

www.thinkfun.com – website of Bill Ritchie and
ThinkFun Inc.

**MAZE-RELATED
MECHANICAL PUZZLES**

(All the following are the creations of
ThinkFun Inc.)

River Crossing®, designed by Andrea Gilbert

Rush Hour®, designed by Nob Yoshigahara

TIPOVER®, designed by James W. Stephens

Amaze™, designed by Eldon Vaughn

Lunar Lockout, designed by Hiroshi Yamamoto
and Nob Yoshigahara

MAZE AND LABYRINTH ORGANIZATIONS

Caerdroia Journal
Jeff Saward, Editor, Caerdroia,
53 Thundersley Grove, Thundersley,
Benfleet, Essex, SS7 3EB, England

www.labyrinthos.net

Dutch Cube Club
Rik van Grol, van Hilvoordestraat 14, 2284
BK Rijswijk, The Netherlands
www.cff.hpage.net

Labyrinth Society
Dr Kimberly Lowelle Saward, President,
P.O. Box 736, Trumansburg, NY 14886, USA
www.labyrinthsociety.org

ThinkFun Inc.
Bill Ritchie, CEO. Andrea Barthello, Founder.
1321 Cameron St. Alexandria, VA 22314
USA, www.thinkfun.com.

Veriditas
The Rev. Dr. Lauren Artress, Founder,
1009 General Kennedy Avenue, 1st Floor
The Presidio, San Francisco, CA 94129, USA
www.veriditas.net

NOTABLE MAZE PROJECTS BY ADRIAN FISHER

HEDGE MAZES

Alice-in-Wonderland Maze, Dorset, England
Bamboo Maze, Alnwick Water Gardens,
Northumberland, England
Blackpool Pleasure Beach, England
Blenheim Palace, Oxfordshire, England
Capel Manor, Hertfordshire, England
Castle Loucen, Czech Republic
Château de Colombier, France
Château de Thoiry, near Paris, France
Cheju Island, South Korea
Dobbies Garden World, Atherstone, England
Escot Park, Devon, England
Leeds Castle, Kent, England
Legoland, Windsor, Berkshire, England
Newquay Zoo, Cornwall, England
Parc Meli Theme Park, Belgium
Portman Lodge, Durweston, Dorset, England
Russborough House, Ireland
Scone Palace, Perth, Scotland
Sigurta Gardens, Italy
Staunton Country Park, Hampshire, England
Three Lands Point Maze, Vaals, Netherlands

MIRROR MAZES

Amsterdam Dungeon, Netherlands
Edinburgh Dungeon, Scotland
Grand Gateway Entertainment Centre,
Shanghai, China

Hamburg Dungeon, Germany
Ibn Battuta Mall, Dubai, UAE
London Dungeon, England
Longleat House, Wiltshire, England
Louis Tussauds, Blackpool, England
Mackinaw City, Michigan, USA
Navy Pier, Chicago, Illinois, USA
Peaugres Safari Park, France
Prasad IMAX Theatre, Hyderabad, India
Ripleys Mirror Maze, Pattaya, Thailand
Seibu Park, Japan
Skyline Caverns, Virginia, USA
Wookey Hole Caves, Somerset, England
York Dungeon, England

PATH-IN-GRASS MAZES

Bath Festival Maze, Bath, Avon, England
Goswells Park, Windsor, Berkshire, England
Greys Court, Oxfordshire, England
Higginson Park, Marlow, Buckinghamshire
Lappa Valley Railway, Cornwall, England
Parham Park, West Sussex, England
Thorpe Park, Surrey, England (no longer exists)
Water Tower Gardens, Chester, England

PAVING MAZES

Cliff School, Wakefield, England
County Mall, Crawley, West Sussex, England
Edinburgh Zoo, Scotland
Kentwell Hall, Suffolk, England

Leicester University, England
Mall of Georgia, Atlanta, Georgia, USA
Mary Hare Grammar School for the Deaf,
Berkshire
Moordown St John's School, Bournemouth,
England
Norton Museum of Art, West Palm Beach,
Florida
Shawford Parish Hall, Hampshire, England
St John's College School, Cambridge, England
Worksop Town Centre, Nottinghamshire,
England

WATER MAZES

Beatles Maze, International Garden Festival,
Liverpool, England, 1984
Castle View Gardens, Jersey, Channel Islands

WOODEN FENCE MAZES

Fort Custer Maze, Ohio, USA
Bicton Park, Devon, England
Holywell Bay Fun Park, Cornwall, England
Legoland, Windsor, Berkshire, England
RNIB New College, Worcester, England

SEASONAL MAIZE MAZES (50 each year)

Arthur's Seat Maze, Victoria, Australia
Belvedere Plantation, Virginia, USA
Davis Megamaze, Sterling, Massachusetts, USA
Ferme de Gally, Versailles, France

ACKNOWLEDGMENTS

Lebanon Valley College, Pennsylvania, USA
Millets Farm Centre, Oxfordshire, England
Red House Farm, Cheshire, England
Rodden Farm, Dorset, England
Tulleys Farm, Turner's Hill, West Sussex, England
Vermont Teddy Bear Company, Shelburne, USA

'SIX MINUTE' MAZES AT SCIENCE
    CENTRES & CHILDREN'S MUSEUMS
Bogota Children's Museum, Colombia,
    South America
Boston Museum of Science, USA

Chicago Museum of Science and Industry, USA
Creative Discovery Museum, Chattanooga, USA
Eureka Children's Museum, Halifax, England
Exploratory Science Centre, Bristol, England
Great Explorations 'Hands-on' Children's
    Museum, Florida, USA
Hamilton Science Centre, New Zealand
Laredo Children's Museum, Texas, USA
Louisiana Children's Museum, New
    Orleans, USA
New York Hall of Science, USA
Pacific Science Center, Seattle, USA

San Antonio Children's Museum, Texas, USA
Science City at Union Station, Kansas City, USA
Techniquest Science Centre, Cardiff, Wales
Wol-Ha Children's Museum, Mexico

PAST MAZE EVENTS AND EXHIBITIONS
Hampton Court Palace, Surrey, England
Norton Museum of Art, West Palm Beach,
    Florida, USA
Oxo Gallery, London, England
State Museum of Pennsylvania, Harrisburg, USA

ACKNOWLEDGMENTS

To each new maze owner, who has participated in the act of creation and made possible the development of this unusual art – this book is their gallery.

To my wife Marie, who shares this joyful livelihood and by her spirit, enthusiasm and determination has transformed our company; our children Felicity, Katharine, Julian, Aidan, Monica and Wilfred, who over the years have unwittingly provided many telling insights into behaviour in mazes; and Robin Fisher, William Fisher and my parents for their lifelong encouragement.

To the late Randoll Coate, fellow explorer of so many early maze design adventures; Peter Haylings, with whom I developed the world's first modern mirror maze; Jeff Saward, founder of the Caerdroia Project; Dudley Heesom and Ann Norris for their perceptive early encouragement; Tom Meldrum for his practical advice and experience; Peter Reid for his business advice and guidance; Marya Lenn Yee, Jacquie McNulty and Ken Roman for their positive encouragement.

To the members of staff, suppliers and contractors of Adrian Fisher Mazes Ltd, past and present, without whose teamwork these hundreds of mazes could not have been created; and in particular Maria Halliday, Tom Hockaday, Nadia Barwani, Nigel Searle, Marilyn Joslin, Angus Mewse, Judy Gentis, Lynda Adby, Paul Kirkman, Jarek Sztandera, Roz MacLean, Sheridan Blackburn, Peter Palmer, Geoff Healing, Drew Cunliffe and Ann Benson. Peter Knight, literary agent and dear friend; Peter Simone, David Ellis and Susan Shapiro, splendid people to work with; Stuart Beare, Larry Davis, Paul Swaffield, Donny Fulks and Jonathan Hewitt, particularly wonderful farmers; dear puzzle enthusiasts Kate Jones, Laurie Brokenshire, Andrea Gilbert, Oskar van Deventer, Ed Pegg, Scott Kim, Jerry Slocum, Tom Rodgers, Robert Abbott, Nick Baxter, Steve Ryan and so many others at the Gatherings for Gardner and International Puzzle Parties. Dick Balfour and the Worshipful Company of Gardeners of London. Roberta Perry, Gene Jeffers, Nick Farmer and others of the Themed Entertainment Association for their worldwide encouragement and fellowship.

PICTURE ACKNOWLEDGMENTS

All illustrations are © Adrian Fisher Mazes Ltd, apart from the following, which are supplied courtesy of Jeff Saward/www.labyrinthos.net: pages 7, 8 left, 24, 26 bottom, 27 top, 28 top left and right, 30, 31, 38 top, 41 top, 80, 85 top and bottom, 92 left and right, 93, 104, 106, 219